Configuration Management with Chef-Solo

A comprehensive guide to get you up and running
with Chef-Solo

Naveed ur Rahman

[PACKT] open source*
PUBLISHING   community experience distilled

BIRMINGHAM - MUMBAI

Configuration Management with Chef-Solo

First published: June 2014

Production reference: 1190614

Published by Packt Publishing Ltd.
Livery Place
35 Livery Street
Birmingham B3 2PB, UK.

ISBN 978-1-78398-246-2

www.packtpub.com

Cover image by Béchir Charfi (charfi.bechir@gmail.com)

Credits

Author
Naveed ur Rahman

Reviewers
Anirudh Bhatnagar

Stuart Ellis

Jorge Moratilla

Commissioning Editor
Edward Gordon

Acquisition Editor
Subho Gupta

Content Development Editor
Sriram Neelakantan

Technical Editors
Venu Manthena

Shruti Rawool

Copy Editors
Janbal Dharmaraj

Karuna Narayanan

Project Coordinator
Aboli Ambardekar

Proofreaders
Maria Gould

Paul Hindle

Indexer
Rekha Nair

Graphics
Disha Haria

Production Coordinator
Shantanu Zagade

Cover Work
Shantanu Zagade

About the Author

Naveed ur Rahman is a self-taught programmer and an avid traveler. When he is not experimenting with the latest in programming and deployment, he is out camping and watching cricket.

His adventures in programming began at a very young age when he got introduced to GW-BASIC. Now, he has experience working for one of the biggest tech names in the Middle East.

Having worked at the largest technology company in the Middle East, Naveed has helped teams create and deploy applications written in various languages using configuration management tools.

I would like to thank my family for supporting me throughout the process of writing. Also, the help of Packt Publishing staff has been incredible. I would like to thank my project coordinator and content development editor who supported me in writing and finalizing the content. Also, the technical reviewers provided me with a clear guideline to make this book more effective. Moreover, their valuable critiques allowed me to refine my work.

About the Reviewers

Anirudh Bhatnagar is a technology consultant with an extensive experience in Agile product development and consulting. He started his career working as a Java developer with product-based companies such as Adobe Systems, India, where most of his experience was in Java, J2EE, Spring, Hibernate, XML, Web Services, REST, CMS, SSO, ESB, and Liferay. Currently, he is working as a Principal Consultant in Xebia, India with specialization in Continuous Delivery methodology, and working on developing a PaaS for service orchestration using Mule ESB, ActiveMQ, Elasticsearch, Jenkins, Maven, Chef, and AWS. He has been contributing to the software community through his blogs, articles, projects, meetups, and conferences. Recently, he has started a DevOps community in New Delhi and has spoken at DevOpsDays India 2013.

Stuart Ellis works for a Ruby on Rails and mobile software development company, where he has many hats. In his current and previous roles, he has developed software with .NET and Ruby, written SQL in a surprising number of dialects, managed different combinations of Windows and Linux, and studied history.

Jorge Moratilla has a Bachelor's degree in Computer Science and has been working for Internet companies since 1998. He has been working as a contractor for companies such as Sun Microsystems and Oracle, working as a certified instructor and field engineer for several years. He has a large background working with technologies and products such as Linux, Solaris, LDAP, and Check Point. Recently, he has been working in development companies, mainly as a system administrator, and performing several tasks related with Agile management, testing, and Continuous Deployment. As a coordinator of the technical group Madrid DevOps, he promotes the adoption of a culture of continuous improvement in the enterprise. You can meet him at talks and hangouts he organizes in the community.

I would like to personally thank my wife Nuria and son Eduardo for being so understanding and supportive while I was reviewing this book. Also, I would like to thank my dear mom Milagros and dad Toñi, who put in all the effort to give me an education. Finally, I would thank also all those who have contributed to my personal and professional development through the years.

www.PacktPub.com

Support files, eBooks, discount offers, and more

You might want to visit www.PacktPub.com for support files and downloads related to your book.

Did you know that Packt offers eBook versions of every book published, with PDF and ePub files available? You can upgrade to the eBook version at www.PacktPub.com and as a print book customer, you are entitled to a discount on the eBook copy. Get in touch with us at service@packtpub.com for more details.

At www.PacktPub.com, you can also read a collection of free technical articles, sign up for a range of free newsletters and receive exclusive discounts and offers on Packt books and eBooks.

http://PacktLib.PacktPub.com

Do you need instant solutions to your IT questions? PacktLib is Packt's online digital book library. Here, you can access, read and search across Packt's entire library of books.

Why subscribe?

- Fully searchable across every book published by Packt
- Copy and paste, print and bookmark content
- On demand and accessible via web browser

Free access for Packt account holders

If you have an account with Packt at www.PacktPub.com, you can use this to access PacktLib today and view nine entirely free books. Simply use your login credentials for immediate access.

Table of Contents

Preface

Chef-Solo is an open source version of chef-client originally developed by Chef Software, Inc. It is a complete framework to automate infrastructure operations for building servers or applications from scratch or adding new configurations to existing systems. These servers are managed by code written in Ruby and it also provides the facility to test and reproduce.

The book will take the reader through the workflow of managing one or more servers. Also, it includes many sample recipes to help you get started.

Throughout the process, we will have a look at the different interaction points and you will learn how Chef-Solo helps to minimize your efforts to build and efficiently manage different machines. You will be able to handle one or more servers from the code written in Ruby. This book will also help you to understand the need for a configuration management tool and an in-depth explanation of Chef-Solo.

This book will provide clear instructions to the reader on how to convert your infrastructure into code. Also, it explains different virtual machines and certain deployment automation tools including Vagrant and Docker.

What this book covers

Chapter 1, *Introduction to Chef and Chef-Solo*, explains about Chef, chef-client, and Chef-Solo. It explains about the core concepts in Chef and the terminologies with some use cases.

Chapter 2, *Setting Up an Environment for Chef-Solo*, guides you to install Chef-Solo on your Ubuntu machine, and discusses cookbooks and their structure in detail. It also provides step-by-step instructions on how to run cookbooks using Chef-Solo with custom configurations.

Chapter 3, Setting Up a Development Environment, explains virtual machines and their providers. In this chapter, we will set up the development environment using Vagrant and execute some sample recipes.

Chapter 4, Developing Cookbooks, looks deeper into developing recipes and how to manage the recipes in cookbooks. It also provides more detailed information on metadata, attributes, templates, files, resources, and data bags. Also, it includes some tools to manage and create cookbooks, for example, Knife and Berkshelf.

Chapter 5, More about Cookbooks and Recipes, continues with the last chapter's cookbooks and manages the remaining contents with files and templates. This chapter includes Python/Django cookbooks and information about upstream service.

Chapter 6, Chef-Solo and Docker, covers the installation of Docker and creation of Docker images using Chef-Solo. Also, this chapter includes some recommendations on how to work on recipes of ongoing projects and keep them aligned with Chef-Solo.

What you need for this book

You need only a single Ubuntu machine to get started. This book contains a step-by-step guide to set up a development environment. Once you have successfully installed everything, you can easily reproduce the same on multiple machines.

Who this book is for

This book is for system administrators and system engineers who have an understanding of configuration management tools and infrastructure. It helps you to understand the need for these tools and provides you with a step-by-step guide to maintain your existing infrastructure. It also contains the most frequently used application recipes to get started immediately.

Conventions

In this book, you will find a number of styles of text that distinguish between different kinds of information. Here are some examples of these styles, and an explanation of their meaning.

Code words in text, database table names, folder names, filenames, file extensions, pathnames, dummy URLs, user input, and Twitter handles are shown as follows: "The `solo.rb` file is used to specify all the configuration details."

A block of code is set as follows:

```
{
    "run_list":[
        "recipe[nginx::default]",
        "recipe[git::default]",
    ]
}
```

When we wish to draw your attention to a particular part of a code block, the relevant lines or items are set in bold:

```
# To update
execute "update apt" do
    command "apt-get update --fix-missing"
end
```

Any command-line input or output is written as follows:

```
$ sudo apt-get install curl
```

New terms and **important words** are shown in bold. Words that you see on the screen, in menus or dialog boxes for example, appear in the text like this: "It should display the **Welcome to nginx!** page."

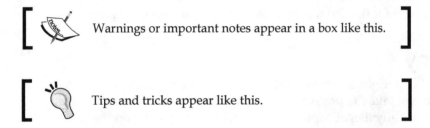

> Warnings or important notes appear in a box like this.

> Tips and tricks appear like this.

Reader feedback

Feedback from our readers is always welcome. Let us know what you think about this book—what you liked or may have disliked. Reader feedback is important for us to develop titles that you really get the most out of.

To send us general feedback, simply send an e-mail to feedback@packtpub.com, and mention the book title via the subject of your message.

If there is a topic that you have expertise in and you are interested in either writing or contributing to a book, see our author guide on www.packtpub.com/authors.

Customer support

Now that you are the proud owner of a Packt book, we have a number of things to help you to get the most from your purchase.

Downloading the example code

You can download the example code files for all Packt books you have purchased from your account at `http://www.packtpub.com`. If you purchased this book elsewhere, you can visit `http://www.packtpub.com/support` and register to have the files e-mailed directly to you.

Errata

Although we have taken every care to ensure the accuracy of our content, mistakes do happen. If you find a mistake in one of our books—maybe a mistake in the text or the code—we would be grateful if you would report this to us. By doing so, you can save other readers from frustration and help us improve subsequent versions of this book. If you find any errata, please report them by visiting `http://www.packtpub.com/submit-errata`, selecting your book, clicking on the **errata submission form** link, and entering the details of your errata. Once your errata are verified, your submission will be accepted and the errata will be uploaded on our website, or added to any list of existing errata, under the Errata section of that title. Any existing errata can be viewed by selecting your title from `http://www.packtpub.com/support`.

Piracy

Piracy of copyright material on the Internet is an ongoing problem across all media. At Packt, we take the protection of our copyright and licenses very seriously. If you come across any illegal copies of our works, in any form, on the Internet, please provide us with the location address or website name immediately so that we can pursue a remedy.

Please contact us at `copyright@packtpub.com` with a link to the suspected pirated material.

We appreciate your help in protecting our authors, and our ability to bring you valuable content.

Questions

You can contact us at `questions@packtpub.com` if you are having a problem with any aspect of the book, and we will do our best to address it.

1
Introduction to Chef and Chef-Solo

Chef is a configuration management system to automate the process of deploying servers to any physical, virtual, or cloud location. Each setup involves the basic structure with one Chef server and different nodes managed by the chef-client. Chef infrastructure is managed by Ruby code and it allows you to test, build, and replicate your infrastructure.

This chapter will guide you through the basics of Chef and how it can help you in building an infrastructure. We will discuss Chef, Chef-Solo, and address some common problems in building an infrastructure and how Chef can help us to solve these problems.

We will cover the following topics in this chapter:

- Chef explanations and concepts
- Chef-Solo
- Terminology for Chef
- Different use cases
- Concepts

Getting started with Chef

Chef is a complete framework to automate infrastructure operations to build servers or applications from scratch or add new configurations to existing systems. Servers are managed by code, written in Ruby and it provides the facility to test and reproduce machines.

Chef basic infrastructure contains at least one server and one node. Each node is maintained and set up by chef-client and is responsible for executing recipes and configuring environments to run applications. It contains the abstract-level configuration of a server or an application.

Tiny code blocks in recipes contain a set of commands that execute on a system sequentially, and gradually configure the whole environment. The complete process is fully automated and without human administration; Chef can set up several nodes.

For instance, if you want 100 servers with Python/Django running Nginx with uWSGI and you want to have the same installations on each node, Chef can make this happen in minutes; it also provides you with the switch to turn your nodes on and off. It can check for revision control system and is responsible for pulling recent updates from the repository. You can easily revert the system to the previous state if something does not happen according to your needs. With Chef, system administrators can spend less time on maintenance and more time on innovation.

Traditional infrastructure is slow and tedious; it involves many steps to build servers and running applications. All your configurations are in one place and you will not worry about the several configurations of different servers. While scaling your application, it is highly recommended to use Chef, as you can easily split your app on to different servers by using roles and nodes. You do not have to install the same application 10 times on one machine or any other, just create a new node in Chef server and in a few minutes, the server will be ready to handle the application. Also, there is no need to maintain the documentation of servers, as the recipes' code is self-explanatory and easy to grasp for a new user.

Chef is developed by Chef Software, Inc. and recently they released Version 11.0. Chef code is completely rewritten in Version 11.0, swapping out Apache CouchDB for PostgreSQL and Ruby for Erlang. The result is massive and now a single Chef server can handle more than 1000 nodes (clients).

Chef is provided in the following three versions:

- **Private Chef**: This is an enterprise version that supports multi-tenancy to provide a highly scalable server to handle several nodes. It should be located in the client's premises and managed behind a firewall.

- **Hosted Chef**: This is an SAAS service managed by Chef Software, Inc. It is a cloud-based service and highly available (24/7 x 365), with roles and resource-based access controls. It does not require a firewall.

- **Open source Chef**: This is a community-driven version with almost identical features, and it should be managed locally and behind the firewall. The latest features initially were released for the commercial version and then gradually released in the open source version. The system administrator will be responsible for applying updates, defining roles, data migrations, and ensuring that the infrastructure scales appropriately.

Chef has been primarily divided into the following three parts:

- **Chef server**: Chef server is responsible for handling nodes and providing cookbooks to clients.

- **chef-client**: The chef-client actually executes the recipes and configures the system. It also resolves each application dependency. The Chef architecture is based on the *Thin server, Thick client* model. There is no need for continuous communication with the server, as the client retrieves the cookbooks from the server and processes recipes on the client end. The server distributes data to each node including cookbooks, templates, files, and other items. The server contains the copy of all items. This approach ensures that each node has persistent data and files.

- **Knife**: Knife is a tool that provides an interface between local-repo and the server. It is used to retrieve cookbooks, policies, roles, environments, and other items.

Understanding Chef-Solo

Chef-Solo is an open source version of chef-client. It executes recipes from the local cookbooks. It is a limited version of chef-client and has much fewer features than it. It does not have the following features:

- **Node data storage**: Node data storage is used to keep values consistent across each node in a large infrastructure.

- **Search indexes**: Search index is a full list of objects that are stored by the server, including roles, nodes, environments, and data bags. They are a fully text-based search and its queries can be made using wildcard, range, and fuzzy logic. While using Knife, a search can be made by using a subcommand from Knife.

  The following command is an example. To search by a platform ID, use the following command:

  ```
  knife search node 'rackspace:*' -i
  ```

The result for the preceding command would be as follows:

```
4 items found
ip-1B45DE89.rackspace.internal
ip-1B45DE89.rackspace.internal
ip-1B45DE89.rackspace.internal
ip-1B45DE89.rackspace.internal
```

> **Downloading the sample code**
>
> You can download the sample code files for all Packt books you have purchased from your account at http://www.packtpub.com. If you purchased this book elsewhere, you can visit http://www.packtpub.com/support and register to have the files e-mailed directly to you.

Similarly, you can search by instance type, node, environment, nested attributes, and multiple arguments.

- **Centralized distribution of cookbooks**: As Chef-Solo works individually, it does not have the ability for distribution of cookbooks. Even if you have deployed Chef server, Chef-Solo will not be able to retrieve recipes from a centralized source.

- **Centralized API for integration with other infrastructure components**: There is no centralized API for Chef-Solo to retrieve other configurations from a different machine. For instance, if your application needs database connectivity, you will not be able to get the IP of the database source. There are multiple solutions to address this problem, which we will discuss in the upcoming chapters.

- **Authentication**: Chef-Solo has no authentication module; anyone can execute the recipes:

```
# chef-solo privileges
test ALL=(ALL) NOPASSWD: /usr/bin/chef-solo
#test is name of non-root user.
```

- **Persistent attributes**: There is no centralized cookbook system for Chef-Solo; it just executes the recipes from a local cookbook.

Although Chef-Solo has fewer features, it provides the core use of developing cookbooks.

Moreover, Chef-Solo provides a simple way to start. You can build the system by using cookbooks and it's extremely useful for booting new machines.

Like chef-client, Chef-Solo can be used for servers, applications, or any physical machine.

Terminologies

We will now discuss some terminologies about Chef. As we have already discussed, Chef has two different types, namely Chef server and Chef-Solo. Chef-Solo provides a simple way to start. The following terminologies mentioned are used for Chef server as well as Chef-Solo.

List of terminologies

A generalized list of Chef terminologies are mentioned in the following section.

Node

Any physical, virtual, or cloud machine where chef-client will run is termed as a node. There are the following four types of nodes that can be managed by chef-client:

- **Cloud node**: This is a server hosted on any cloud-based service such as Rackspace, Amazon, Virtual Private Cloud, OpenStack, Google Compute Engine, or Windows Azure. Different plugins are available for supporting different cloud types. It can be used to create instances using cloud-based services.

- **Physical node**: Physical node is a server or a virtual machine that has the capability of sending, receiving, and forwarding data through a network channel. In simple words, a network machine that runs the chef-client.

- **Virtual node**: A virtual node runs as a software implementation but behaves like a proper machine, for example, VirtualBox, Docker, and so on.

- **Network node**: This is a device attached to the network and capable of sending, receiving, and forwarding data, and managed by chef-client. Routers, switches, and firewalls are a perfect example of network nodes.

Workstation

A workstation is a machine, where Knife configures and sends instructions to a node. Knife is used to manage nodes, cookbooks and recipes, roles, and environments. A commercial Knife version can be used to search index data on the server.

For a production environment, workstation authentication is managed by RSA or a DSA key pair. Authentication ensures that a workstation is properly registered with the server.

Moreover, Chef-repo is maintained on the workstation and it is distributed in chef-clients from the workstation. Once the distribution is done, chef-client executes the recipes and installs everything on the system.

Cookbooks

Cookbooks are a collection of recipes. Each cookbook defines the policy and scenario to install and configure any particular machine. For instance, installing PostgreSQL needs `libpq-dev` and other packages. It contains all the components that need to be installed on the system.

Additional configurations can be set up using cookbooks:

- Attributes to set on nodes
- Definitions of resources
- Dependency control
- File distributions
- Libraries to help Chef-Solo to extend Ruby code, for example, Berkshelf, Librarian-Chef
- Templates
- Custom resources and providers
- Roles
- Metadata of recipes
- Versions

Cookbooks are written in Ruby code. It's good to have knowledge about Ruby, but it's not mandatory. The Ruby code used in cookbooks is very simple and self-explanatory. While using cookbooks, you do not need to maintain the documentation of the server setup.

The sole purpose of a cookbook is to give a reasonable set of resources to a chef-client for the infrastructure automation.

Recipes

Recipes are the fundamental configuration elements in cookbooks. A recipe contains a set of commands that needs to be executed step by step. A recipe can include additional recipes within a recipe.

Each code block contains a set of instructions. For example, take a look at the following code:

```
# To update
execute "update apt" do
  command "apt-get update --fix-missing"
end

# For installing some packages
%w{
    curl
    screen
    make
    python2.7-dev
    vim
    python-setuptools
    libmysqlclient-dev
    mysql-client
}.each do |pkg|
  package pkg do
    action :install
  end
end
```

Recipes are written in Ruby code, and it contains the set of resources; each code block is wrapped in a resource. In the previous example, `execute` and `package` is a resource to handle code inside a block.

There are certain rules for writing recipes:

- It should maintain a proper order. For instance, if you want to use MySQL, you must specify the `libmysqlclient-dev` package first and then install MySQL.
- Recipes must be placed in the `cookbook` folder.
- It must define everything that needs to be installed in a particular environment.
- Recipes must be declared in `run_list` to execute in any recipe.
- Any additional recipe that you specify should be contained in the same `cookbook` folder or you should have some dependency resolved to include the recipe (Berkshelf allows you to include the recipe from `github.com`).

Resources

A resource is an integral part of any recipe. It defines the actions to be taken in a recipe. It could be a service, a package, a group of a user, and so on. For example, it will instruct chef-client to check whether a particular package needs to be installed or not, or when a service needs to be restarted or not, and which directory or file needs to be created by which user. Each resource is written in a code block and it executes in the same order as mentioned in the recipe. Chef-Solo ensures that each action has to be taken as specified in the recipe. After the successful execution of resources, it returns the success code to chef-client. In case there is an error, it returns with an error code and chef-client exits with an error.

The following is an example of a directory resource:

```
directory "/var/log/project" do
  owner "root"
  group "root"
  recursive true
  action :create
end
```

The chef-client will look up the directory resource and call `load_current_resource` to create a new directory resource. The client will look up the directory; if it's not created, it will create the directory in the `logs` folder, and if the directory already exists, nothing will happen and the resource will be marked as completed.

The following is an example of a Git resource:

```
git "/home/user/webapps/project" do
  repository "git@github.com:opscode-cookbooks/chef_handler.git"
  reference "master"
  action :sync
  enable_submodules true
  user "root"
  group "root"
end
```

The mentioned Git resource will pull the code from the repository with all sub-modules.

It will switch the branch to master and async will ensure that recent changes have been pulled from the remote repository to the local repository.

The resource is mainly divided into the following four parts:

- Type
- Name
- Attributes
- Actions

The coding convention of the resource is shown in the following code:

```
resourcetype "name" do
    attribute "value"
    action :action
end
```

In the preceding code, `resourcetype` is the name of a resource, for example, directory, file, apache_site, and so on.

As we have discussed earlier that each resource has separate actions, the `action` command is used to execute these actions.

Each resource has its own type of actions and attributes. The `directory` resource has a `create` and a `delete` action. Each resource has its own default actions and attributes. Similarly, the default action directory resource is `create`. And it has `group`, `inherits`, `mode`, `owner`, `path`, `provider`, `recursive`, and `right` attributes.

Roles

In simple words, the reusable configuration of several nodes, for example, database, Web, and so on, are called as roles. They define certain patterns and processes that need to be installed in different nodes. When a role runs against any recipe, attributes have been overwritten with role attributes.

Each node can have zero or more roles assigned to it and then `run_list` of roles will be executed on the node.

An attribute can be defined both in a node and in a role. Role should have at least the following attributes:

- `name`: This attribute gives the name of the role
- `description`: This contains the description of the role
- `run_list`: Recipes need to be executed with this role

Roles can be declared in two ways: we can define it in Ruby or in JSON. In case of JSON, there are some additional attributes, such as `chef_type`, `json_class` that need to be defined. Detailed information about roles is available in the next chapter.

Attributes

In simple terms, attributes are variables that are defined in a cookbook to be used by recipes and templates to create configuration files. When chef-client executes the recipes, it loads all the attributes from cookbooks, recipes, and roles.

Attributes are declared in the `attributes` folder under cookbooks. When any recipe is executed, it checks within the context of the current node and applies on that node.

For example, Nginx cookbook attributes are given as follows:

```
default["nginx"]["dir"]          = "/etc/nginx"
default["nginx"]["listen_ports"] = [ "80","443" ]
```

Similarly, Git attributes are given as follows:

```
default["project"][:project_path] = "/home/chef/webapps/project"
default["project"][:repository] = "git@github.com:opscode-cookbooks/
chef_handler.git"
```

We have already discussed about the attributes' precedence in the *Roles* section. We will discuss attributes in more detail in the upcoming chapters.

Templates

A template is a simple configuration file that has a placeholder for attributes. Templates files are written in Embedded Ruby (`.erb`) format. For example, to deploy Nginx, you need the `nginx.conf.erb` file.

A sample of a template file is mentioned as follows:

```
server {
    listen 80;
    server_name <%= node["project"]["domain"] %>;
    access_log <%= node["project"]["logs_dir"] %>/<%= node["project"]
["project"_name] %>_access.log;
    error_log <%= node["project"]["logs_dir"] %>/<%= node["project"]
["project"_name] %>_error.log;
    location / {
        client_max_body_size 20M;
        client_body_temp_path /tmp/
        expires -1;
        proxy_pass          http://localhost:8000;
        proxy_set_header    X-Real-IP  $remote_addr;
        send_timeout 5m;
        keepalive_timeout 5m;
        gzip on;
    }
}
```

In the preceding example, the following attributes will be replaced and the configuration file will be copied to a specific directory with a real value:

```
node["project"]["domain"] = "http://mydomain.com"
node["project"]["logs_dir"] = "/var/logs/project"
```

Data bags

A data bag is a global variable defined in JSON and accessible from a server.

The following is an example:

```
{
    "project": {
        "dbdomain": "dbdomain.com",
        "dbuser": "database_user",
        "dbpassword": "database_password"
    },
    "run_list": [
        "recipe[git::default]",
        "recipe[nginx::default]",
        "recipe[project::default]"
    ]
}
```

In the preceding example, Dbdomain, dbuser, and dbpassword are the data bags.

Different use cases

The best way to learn Chef is to see real-world examples. We will not install and create nodes in the current chapter, but we will explain the dependencies of different environments. More detailed information about installation of these environments will be explained in *Chapter 2, Setting Up an Environment for Chef-Solo*.

PHP WordPress

This section assumes that you are already familiar with WordPress. To set up a WordPress site, we need the following packages installed on any machine:

- Apache Web server
- MySQL Database server
- PHP

Chef-Solo will be responsible for downloading WordPress and configuring Apache and PHP along with its dependencies. Chef Software, Inc. already has a WordPress recipe. We can use the same recipe to install a new blog.

Python/Django application

In this example, we will configure a node for Python application, assuming our Python application is built in Python using a Django framework with a MySQL database.

To run the web server, we will use Nginx. The complete requirements will look like the following:

- Python
- Django framework
- Nginx

As you can see, quite a long list needs to be installed on a system to work properly. After defining the recipes, all the instructions are written in code files and after execution of these recipes, the server will be up and running.

Chef provides us with the facility to automate to achieve efficiency, scalability, reusability, and documentation.

An overview of Chef

The idea of Chef is to automate the whole process; it is rare that any single individual knows everything in such a large infrastructure. Also, Chef has a large community that participates to solve large problems.

The basic principle of Chef is that the user knows each bit of the environment; for example which are the packages that need to be installed, requirements of your applications, and so on. The best person for any application development is the team who developed the system. While creating a system, they can write down the requirements and easily convert them into Ruby code.

Moreover, any large organization uses a number of different packages to handle web applications, for instance, you have a Python application, running on Nginx, using uWSGI, caching with memcahe and redis, and using Elasticsearch for quick search.

All the mentioned packages have a list of dependencies. Once you have the recipes, you can run them once or several times on the same system and the results will be identical. The chef-client keeps track of the changes in resources. If any resource item is updated, then it runs the resource again and marks it as successful.

Chef is designed on a *Thin Server, Thick Client* approach. The client does not need continuous communication to the server. Once the client receives the set of instructions (cookbooks), it will execute and report to the server. The server is responsible for the distribution of cookbooks, templates, environments, and so on, via the workstation. Also, the server will keep a copy of all configurations.

Moreover, while creating the recipes, an order should be maintained. As we have already discussed, recipes are based on several resources. Each resource contains a set of actions and are executed one by one. The resources execute sequentially and the order needs to be maintained. For example, if you try to install PostgreSQL before `libpq-dev`, you will get the error of missing dependency and the recipe script will exit with an error.

Summary

In this chapter, we have discussed Chef, chef-client, and Chef-Solo. We also discussed some core concepts of Chef and had a look at different use cases. Also, we elaborated upon certain Chef terminologies such as nodes, workstations, cookbooks, recipes, resources, roles, attributes, templates, and data bags.

In the next chapter, we will discuss the cookbooks in more detail and set up a Linux machine with Chef, and will execute some open source recipes.

2
Setting Up an Environment for Chef-Solo

We have already discussed some brief theory about Chef-Solo in the previous chapter, but we can't get anywhere until we've installed Chef-Solo and have had a hands-on experience with Chef.

This chapter will guide you with a step-by-step installation of Chef-Solo. We need some additional packages to get it working. Also, we will have a look into the configurations to get it working.

We will cover the following topics in this chapter:

- Installation on Linux and Ubuntu
- Prerequisites of Chef-Solo
- Chef-Solo cookbook
- Configurations
- Downloading a few sample cookbooks
- Execution of the recipes

Installation on Linux and Ubuntu

Chef provides us with a number of ways to get started. We can get it working using different methods. Each method has certain advantages and disadvantages. Chef-Solo can be installed as a Ruby gem, or a Debian package and is not available as **Red Hat Package Manager (RPM)** packages for Red Hat based Linux.

The detailed installation methods are discussed in the following sections.

Installing Chef as a Ruby gem

Chef is written in Ruby, and before getting started with Chef-Solo, we have to install Ruby. The installation is simple enough and it requires only two packages to get started. Ruby developers may prefer this particular method to get started.

```
apt-get install Ruby1.9.3 Ruby1.9.3-dev build-essential
```

This will install Ruby Version 1.9.1 and also a few required extensions. After installation of Ruby, we can easily install Chef using it as a Ruby gem. We can install Ruby by using the following snippet:

```
gem1.9.3 install --no-ri --no-rdoc chef
```

Also, you can install different versions of Chef with different versions of Ruby.

For a development machine, that is about all you will need apart from a cookbook, and some dependencies.

The advantages of installing Chef as a Ruby gem are as follows:

- It is a simple method and easier to implement. Ruby developers ideally prefer this method to get started.

- It uses the commonly used Ruby libraries and gems (extensions), and you have to rely on Ruby gem globally.

- As we have already discussed, Chef-Solo will use globally used Ruby libraries, and your recipes can use any gem installed on your system.

The disadvantages of installing Chef as a Ruby gem are as follows:

- As Ruby has a very mature system of **Ruby Version Manager** (**RVM**), some developers are not very comfortable with the Ruby version globally in use as RVM enables you to have multiple Ruby environments on the same system, each having different Ruby versions and software.

- Ruby gem is not installed as a system package. It can work well in a system globally, but cannot be integrated with the operating system package manager. Different operating systems provide different methods to handle the packages.

Also, a system wide Ruby installation and a Ruby gem will not ensure that your recipes will work perfectly with specific gem versions. For instance, if your recipe is dependent on x-gem 2, an x-gem 3 can break your recipe.

Please note that `apt-get` package manager is available for Ubuntu, and similarly, Yum is available for Red Hat.

Installing Chef as a package manager

Installing Chef as a package manager method installs Chef-Solo using **Opscode** (Chef was originally developed by Opscode) published packages for different distributions and operating systems. The process is pretty straightforward. The steps are as follows:

1. Add the Opscode repository to your system.

2. Create the new file as `/etc/apt/sources.list.d/opscode.list` or edit the mentioned file `/etc/apt/sources.list`.

3. All the distributions are listed at `http://apt.opscode.com/conf/distributions`:

   `deb http://apt.opscode.com/ <codename>-0.10 main`

4. Fetch and trust the Opscode GPG key. Install the `opscode-keyring` package for auto updates by using the following commands:

   ```
   $ sudo wget -O- http://apt.opscode.com/packages@opscode.com.gpg.
   key | sudo apt-key add -
   ```
   ```
   $ sudo apt-get update
   ```
   ```
   $ sudo apt-get install opscode-keyring
   ```

5. Finally, install Chef by using the following command line:

   ```
   $ sudo apt-get install chef
   ```

The advantages of installing Chef as a package manager are as follows:

* Chef is installed as a package here, and can be easily upgraded using `apt-get upgrade`.

* It can be used as preinstalled on a **virtual machine** (**VM**). We can easily include the package with VM using the `vm-builder` tool.

The disadvantage of installing Chef as a package manager is as follows:

* Adding keys and a PPA repository is a complex method to install any package. It would be great if Chef gets introduced as a complete package.

Using the Omnibus installer

The Omnibus installer is a full installation and an executable script. Thanks to Opscode, they provide the executable script to install packages and dependencies.

Execute the following script by using the following command:

```
$ sudo curl -L https://www.opscode.com/chef/install.sh | bash
```

> Curl utility is not part of Ubuntu. You can install by using the following command:
>
> ```
> $ sudo apt-get install curl
> ```

It will download the recent version and install along with every dependency. Please note that in the background, the `bash` script will download the compatible version and install it. In Ubuntu, you can later use **Debian package management (dpkg)** to see the installed Omnibus packages and remove them if desired. So even with Omnibus, `apt-get purge chef` will work correctly.

The installation will be placed in the `/opt/chef` folder and it will contain a full Ruby installation in the `/opt/chef/embedded` folder.

The advantages of the Omnibus installer are as follows:

- Personally, I prefer using this method as it involves very simple and easy steps to install Chef. I have been using it on different machines with great success as it isolates the Ruby environment and there will not be much of a chance to break the recipes.
- It provides a complete debian package. And later, you can upgrade it or remove it with a system package manager.

The disadvantage of the Omnibus installer is as follows:

- Third-party gem installation will be difficult and while executing the recipes, we need to use a full path (if the path is not included in the global path, you can always add the `gem` directory in the `path` variable)

Prerequisites of Chef-Solo

We already discussed about installation setups for Chef-Solo. If you are using the Omnibus method, you don't need to worry about any dependencies. However, for installation as a Ruby gem or package management, please ensure that the following packages are installed on your machine.

Use the following command to install the required packages:

```
$ sudo apt-get install Ruby1.9.3 build-essential
```

For Omnibus, make sure `curl` is installed on your machine:

```
$ sudo apt-get install curl
```

 curl is a command-line tool for transferring data with URL syntax. It supports various protocols including HTTP, FTP, and FTPS.

Some dependencies for Berkshelf are as follows:

```
$ sudo apt-get install libxslt-dev libxml2-dev openssl zlib1g
```

To ensure that Chef-Solo installs correctly, go to the terminal and write the following command:

```
$ chef-solo -v
```

The preceding command will display the Chef version as shown in the following screenshot:

```
naveed@lenovo: ~
naveed@lenovo:~$ chef-solo -v
Chef: 11.10.4
naveed@lenovo:~$
```

Cookbooks

Cookbooks are a collection of recipes and they consist of basic and fundamental units of various policies and distributions. Each cookbook contains complete setups to install every distribution on a machine.

For instance, we need a web server, so we are installing Nginx to act as a web server. The Nginx cookbook should contain all the package names that are dependent to install Nginx. Moreover, it should provide step-by-step instructions to the machine to make this happen.

Let's have a detailed look at how to develop a cookbook.

The folder structure

Cookbooks should ideally consist of the following folder structure. As they are a collection of different recipes, while executing the recipe by default, Chef-Solo will look for a default folder:

```
attributes
    default.rb
files
    default
        file.txt
recipes
    default.rb
templates
    default
        file.erb
metadata.rb
```

Attributes

As we have already discussed about these terminologies in the last chapter here, once again, we will discuss the role of each file.

In the `attributes` directory, the `default.rb` file will be used to declare all variables that we are going to use in the execution of recipes given out in the following code:

```
default['nginx']['version']       = '1.4.4'
default['nginx']['package_name']  = 'nginx'
default['nginx']['dir']           = '/etc/nginx'
default['nginx']['script_dir']    = '/usr/sbin'
default['nginx']['log_dir']       = '/var/log/nginx'
```

The code that is used here is taken from the Opscode Nginx recipe available at `https://github.com/opscode-cookbooks/nginx`.

Variables are declared in the Ruby syntax. Now throughout the recipe, we can use `default['nginx']['version']` to get the version of Nginx.

All `.rb` files support the Ruby syntax, so we can use control structures for conditional declarations. In the following example, we are selecting an `nginx` user as per platform:

```ruby
case node['platform_family']
when 'debian'
  default['nginx']['user']       = 'www-data'
  default['nginx']['init_style'] = 'runit'
when 'rhel', 'fedora'
  default['nginx']['user']        = 'nginx'
  default['nginx']['init_style']  = 'init'
  default['nginx']['repo_source'] = 'epel'
when 'gentoo'
  default['nginx']['user']       = 'nginx'
  default['nginx']['init_style'] = 'init'
else
  default['nginx']['user']       = 'www-data'
  default['nginx']['init_style'] = 'init'
end
```

Files

The `files` folder is used to copy the files to your new machine. For instance, if we have a configuration file and want to copy it to a specific location, we will place it in the `files` folder and copy that to a specific directory as mentioned in the recipe.

Recipes

The `recipes` folder is the place where the real magic occurs. In the `recipes` folder, we have a `default.rb` file that contains a set of instructions to install and configure any machine.

For installation on Ubuntu, first we need to update the packages. The following code will be used to update Ubuntu packages. Add the following code block in the recipe:

```ruby
execute "update apt" do
  command "apt-get update"
  ignore_failure true
end
```

After updating systems apt, we need to install some mandatory packages to get started:

```
%w{
    curl
    screen
    vim
    python-setuptools
    libreadline-dev
    libevent-dev
    libpq-dev

}.each do |pkg|
  package pkg do
    action :install
  end
end
```

As we have already discussed about the resources, each resource is responsible for performing a particular scenario.

The previous code installs a few packages. Firstly, it writes all the package names that need to be installed in the `%w{}` block and then, `each do |pkg|` loops through all packages' lists and installs them one by one.

The mentioned resource will install `curl`, `screen`, `make`, `python2.7`, and `vim` packages.

You might have noticed during installation that each resource has different attributes, which can be used to perform a specific action. Similarly, we have a different resource, `git`, for performing Git clone and submodule operations.

Moreover, if we want to execute some shell script, we can do this via the `execute` resource. The following is an example of the `script` resource to install Python packages with **Python Package Manager (pip)**:

```
script "pip_install" do
  interpreter "bash"
  user "root"
  group "root"
  cwd node[:project][:project_path]
  code <<-EOH
    # simple shell code can be written here to execute
  git checkout master
    # assuming we have python requirements file in directory, it can be
used in the recipe by using the following code
  pip install -r requirements.txt
  EOH
end
```

The code block given out in the preceding example will execute as a shell script, check out the preferred branch, and it will also install the Python requirements file. You might have noticed that we have some statements with the # sign. These values are an attribute that we have already seen in the attributes: the `default.rb` file.

Using Git in a `execute` resource is not a recommended practice. Please refer to the Git cookbook and we can use the `git` resource to execute Git commands.

In the following code, we will use one file and copy that to our desired directory:

```
cookbook_file "/home/user/file.txt" do
  source "file.txt"
  owner "root"
  group "root"
end
```

The preceding code block will be responsible to copy `file.txt` in `/home/user/`.

For a list of complete resources and attributes, please refer to the Chef Software, Inc. documentation provided earlier in the chapter.

Templates

Templates are Embedded Ruby (`.erb`) files, by which you can display the attribute values. They are used to create configuration files in our new machine. A sample Nginx configuration file is given out as an example in the following code:

```
server {
  listen    80;
  server_name  <%= node['hostname'] %>;
  access_log  <%= node['nginx']['log_dir'] %>/localhost.access.log;
  location / {
    root  <%= node['nginx']['default_root'] %>;
    index  index.html index.htm;
  }
}
```

> Please refer to the following link for detailed information on ERB files: `http://ruby-doc.org/stdlib2.1.1/libdoc/erb/rdoc/ERB.html`

Sample file contains the basic configuration of the Nginx web server. Attribute `<-= node['hostname']%>` and other attributes will be replaced by the actual value (which we have defined in the `attributes` file).

You may have noticed that we used a default folder or a default file in each instance. So what exactly is *default*? While running the recipe in Chef-Solo, we need to pass a recipe name; chef-client will look for the same name in the mentioned folder. Your cookbook can be a collection of many recipes, imagining you are writing a cookbook for database, and it contains two types of recipes, that is PostgreSQL and MySQL. In this case, we have to create two files in the `Recipes` folder, `postgresql.rb` and `mysql.rb`. Similarly, in attributes, files, and templates, each recipe will look for the same name folder/filename to use as values.

We can maintain one cookbook for different types of database installations. To run a recipe, we will enlist the recipe names in `run_list [database::mysql]` to install MySQL. Chef-Solo will use the files mentioned as follows:

```
attributes
    mysql.rb
files
    mysql
        file.txt
recipes
    mysql.rb
templates
    mysql
        file.erb
```

The `metadata.rb` file contains the name, maintainer information, description, and some dependency information as follows:

```
name              'nginx'
maintainer        'Opscode, Inc.'
description       'Installs and configures nginx'
version           '2.4.3'
recipe 'nginx',   'Installs nginx package and sets up configuration
                  with Debian apache style with sites-enabled/
                  sites-available'
depends 'apt',    '~> 2.2'
```

Downloading recipes

Let's download a few recipes on a test environment and execute them with Chef-Solo.

First, we'll make a folder named `cookbooks` and download the Nginx recipe to execute. As we have already installed Chef-Solo in our working environment, use the following command to create a folder named `cookbooks`:

```
$ mkdir cookbooks && cd cookbooks
$ git clone https://github.com/opscode-cookbooks/nginx
```

Git provides two methods to download repositories to a local storage. We can use Git and/or https protocol to clone the repository. Our main objective is to place cookbooks under the `cookbooks` directory.

Chef-Solo configuration

After having downloaded a few recipes, we want to run those recipes and make the system ready. The `solo.rb` file is used to specify all the configuration details. Its default configuration is loaded every time. By a default configuration, the file exists at `/etc/chef/solo.rb`, but we can use it with a custom path. The `solo.rb` file can contain several settings but mainly it is used for the cookbook's path, data bag's path, environment, environment path, log_location, and so on.

You can read all the detailed information about each configuration at `www.getchef.com`.

Our `solo.rb` file is pretty simple and contains only a few settings.

Create a new `solo.rb` file with the following content:

```
file_cache_path    "/var/chef/cache"
file_backup_path   "/var/chef/backup"
cookbook_path ["/home/<username>/cookbooks"]
# An alternative and more useable method is to use ruby code to get
directory path
    cookbook_path File.expand_path('/cookbooks')
log_level :info
verbose_logging    false
```

Now create another `nginx.json` file (any name can be used) to instruct Chef-Solo to execute the recipe as follows:

```
{
    "run_list": [
        "recipe[nginx::default]"
    ]
}
```

Execution of recipes

Now we have everything in place, let's execute the recipe to install Nginx.

```
$ chef-Solo -c ./solo.rb -j nginx.json
```

Please note that the preceding command will fail with an error because the other required cookbooks are not there. To install an Nginx recipe, we need some other dependent recipes in the `cookbooks` folder.

As you noticed in the Nginx `cookbooks/metadata.rb` file, the Nginx recipe is dependent on the following recipes. Before proceeding, we will download the cookbooks that contain the required recipes within the `cookbooks` folder. In the upcoming chapters, we'll learn how to download and execute recipes with a dependency resolver (for example, Berkshelf):

```
depends 'apt',              '~> 2.2'
depends 'bluepill',         '~> 2.3'
depends 'build-essential',  '~> 1.4'
depends 'ohai',             '~> 1.1'
depends 'runit',            '~> 1.2'
depends 'yum',              '~> 3.0'
depends 'yum-epel'
depends 'rsyslog'
```

After you have downloaded all the preceding recipes (please note that you must download all the dependencies to install Nginx), our folder structure will look like the following:

```
cookbooks
    nginx
    apt
    bluepill
    build-essential
    ohai
    rsyslog
    runit
    yum
    yum-epel
solo.rb
nginx.json
```

Let's download these recipes from Git and execute with Chef-Solo. After completing the recipe, you should be successful and a **service [nginx] started** message will appear, as shown in the following screenshot:

```
Recipe: nginx::default
  * service[nginx] action start[2014-03-11T20:51:45+00:00] INFO: service[nginx] started

    - start service service[nginx]

[2014-03-11T20:51:45+00:00] INFO: template[nginx.conf] sending reload action to service[nginx] (delayed)
  * service[nginx] action reload[2014-03-11T20:51:46+00:00] INFO: service[nginx] reloaded

    - reload service service[nginx]

[2014-03-11T20:51:46+00:00] INFO: Chef Run complete in 14.533680434 seconds

Running handlers:
[2014-03-11T20:51:46+00:00] INFO: Running report handlers
Running handlers complete

[2014-03-11T20:51:46+00:00] INFO: Report handlers complete
Chef Client finished, 10/19 resources updated in 15.922317173 seconds
```

Nginx is installed and ready to use. Cross check if it is installed properly by using the `curl` command or type `localhost` in the browser.

It should display the **Welcome to nginx!** page.

Download some sample cookbooks for Apache2, MySQL, and install them via Chef-Solo. Also, you can install various recipes using one single recipe as shown in the following code snippet:

```
{
    "run_list": [
        "recipe[nginx::default]",
        "recipe[git::default]",
    ]
}
```

Add the recipes in `run_list` and Chef will execute the recipes for you.

Summary

In this chapter, we have installed Chef-Solo on our Ubuntu machine, and discussed it in detail covering cookbooks and their structure. We also covered some step-by-step instructions on how to run cookbooks using Chef-Solo. We also had a look into Chef-Solo custom configuration and used JSON to run recipes.

In the next chapter, we will discuss more in detail about cookbooks and will develop them for a complete system environment (Python, Django, Nginx, MySQL, and uWSGI).

Moreover, we will look into the community maintained recipes to install different apps.

3
Setting Up a Development Environment

In the previous chapter, we installed Chef-Solo on our local environment and executed recipes with Nginx. However, imagine if we were working on different projects and some projects require different web servers and configurations. It would be difficult to install everything on the same system.

In this chapter, we'll install **VirtualBox** with Vagrant to set up our box and execute different recipes in different boxes.

We will cover the following topics in this chapter:

- Introduction to VirtualBox
- Setting up Vagrant
- Executing the Nginx recipe with Vagrant
- Creating a hello world recipe

Introducing virtual machine

Virtual machine is a software implementation that executes and runs an operating system like a physical machine, and any program can run on this new machine.

Virtual machine provides various advantages over the installation of OS. Mainly, virtual machines for different emulators and in cloud-based architecture provide total isolation, and a complete isolation ensures that any services or packages are not affecting your main OS. Moreover, you can easily create, delete, export, and import different environments. Many large hosting providers use virtual machines for backups, disaster recovery, deployments, and administration tasks.

Operating system tasks such as CPU usage, memory, hard disk, and USB are managed by the virtualization layer. The virtualization layer translates these requests to the underlying hardware layer.

Mainly, virtual machines are classified into two levels based on their use. They are explained in the following sections.

System virtual machines

System virtual machines provide a complete operating system, and you can install any software like a real machine. It usually uses the same architecture and is built with a purpose to test or run programs in a real environment. For example, Microsoft provides various versions of Windows with different Internet Explorer versions. Windows virtual machines are used to check the browser compatibility. For instance, we would want to check our site in IE8, IE9, and so on. For this, we can install different VMs on the same machine. Microsoft provides free VMs that are licensed specifically for browser testing, only at http://www.modern.ie/en-us/virtualization-tools. Moreover, in cloud computing, virtual machines are used to provide a platform to run different environments. It is an efficient use of a machine in terms of hardware cost and system effectiveness.

Process virtual machines

A process virtual machine (also called an application virtual machine) executes as a normal application on an operating system and supports only a single process. The purpose of process virtual machines is to provide a platform-independent programming environment that abstracts details of the underlying hardware and transforms an application into a portable software. When an application starts, it will initiate one process, and when it exits, it will destroy the process. It provides a high level of abstraction and can be written in any high-level programming language. Unlike system virtual machine, it allows us to perform specific tasks on an operating system. Good examples of process virtual machines are JVM, Microsoft .NET Framework, and Lua.

Virtual machines were originally defined by Popek and Goldberg as "an efficient, isolated duplicate of a real machine".

There are various software available as system virtual machines. They are as follows:

- **VirtualBox**: VirtualBox offers many features free of charge, supported by Oracle. Configurations (virtual machine's parameters and descriptions) are stored in the XML files. It provides you with an easy interface to export settings from one box to another. It is available for Windows, Linux, and Mac OS at http://www.virtualbox.org/.

- **Parallels**: Parallels is best for Mac, but it is available for Windows and Linux as well. Parallels offers clipboard sharing, synchronization, and shared folders between two machines (like other competitors). When you switch from your base OS to a virtual machine, it automatically increases the processing power to that of the virtual machine. The base price of Parallels is around 80 USD. It is available at `http://www.parallels.com/`.

- **VMware**: VMware provides two kinds of boxes: **VM Player** and **VM Workstation**. VM Player is used for primary purposes and provides a basic functionality to test the basic content in your box. Meanwhile, VM Workstation is a full-fledged box that provides various methods to create, export, and clone a box. Also, it has the capability of hardware optimization, driver-less printing, and so on. At the Enterprise level, it's leading in the industry and costs around 200 USD.

  Also, vSphere is another server solution from VMware. It's a complete suite and has a combination of vCenter, ESXi, vSphere client, and so on.

  For detailed information, please refer to the VMware site at `http://www.vmware.com/`.

- **QEMU-KVM**: QEMU-KVM is a fork of the QEMU project, and it is available for only Linux machines (the latest version is 2.0 RC). It is a powerful system with a built-in Linux kernel-based virtual machine. The main feature of QEMU is that it can execute a guest machine on the host hardware. This means you can carry your box with you and execute it without having administration permissions. Without administration access, it can be used to build thumb-drive-based virtual machines. Thumb-drive-based virtual machines are software that can run on flash drives. For example, Google Chrome, Portable Ubuntu, and so on. And yes, we can use it free of charge.

- **Windows Virtual PC**: This is available only for Windows and offers a very basic functionality. It provides a virtual machine for Windows, and you can install earlier versions of Windows on it. It is designed for user groups that are strictly using the Windows environment and need to test applications on earlier versions.

We'll use the VirtualBox and install Ubuntu Version 12.04 to get started. The installation of VirtualBox is simple. Luckily, VirtualBox is available in the main `apt-get` repository, and we can install it with the following command:

```
$ sudo apt-get install virtualbox
```

If you are using Synaptic on Ubuntu, it will be available in the software list or can be installed by Ubuntu Software Center.

Before running a VirtualBox, please make sure that CPU virtualization is switched on in your BIOS. Please note that not all x86 systems cannot virtualize.

VirtualBox provides various boxes to install different operating systems. The list of the operating systems can be found at the following link:

```
http://virtualboxes.org/images/
```

In our case, we need a box, but we do not actually need a graphical interface to perform individual tasks. We can use some automated deployment tools, such as Vagrant, to add a box (a box is a Vagrant term used to describe any kind of virtual machine that Vagrant manages) and execute our recipes in a new system.

Some advantages of using Vagrant are mentioned in the following points:

- Vagrant is an automated tool that facilitates to automate the virtual environment
- We can manage virtual machines using Vagrant

Vagrant is an open source tool for managing virtual machines. It was developed by Mitchell Hashimoto and John Bender. It can be used to manage virtual machines in VirtualBox, a full x86 virtualizer that is also open source (GPLv2). Initially, it was tied to VirtualBox, but after Version 1.1, it's no longer related to VirtualBox and can be used with VMware and Amazon EC2. The current versions also support Microsoft Hyper-V. There is an optional plugin for Google Compute Engine.

Vagrant provides simple methods to arrange reproducible and transportable work situations. It isolates the dependencies and configurations in a single file. With a single command, your system will be ready to use. Also, it provides a method to execute recipes with a `Vagrantfile`, so your environment will be ready with the `vagrant up` command.

The installation of Vagrant can be done using a Debian package (Debian packages work on both Debian and Ubuntu machines). We need to download the DEB file from `https://www.vagrantup.com/downloads.html`.

Download the version as per your operating system and install it. In our case, we will download the Debian Ubuntu version.

 We need to install the following versions of VirtualBox and Vagrant:

- VirtualBox: 4.3
- Vagrant: 1.5.3

Vagrant has some basic commands that can be used for different purposes. They are elaborated in the following table:

Command	Function
$ vagrant init	This creates a basic configuration file with default settings
$ vagrant up	This starts a new machine as settings defined in Vagrantfile (the configuration file for a Vagrant project)
$ vagrant suspend	This suspends the running guest
$ vagrant halt	This stops the running machine and sends a shutdown signal to the machine
$ vagrant resume	This resumes the Vagrant machine that was suspended earlier
$ vagrant reload	This reloads the current guest
$ vagrant status	This is used to check the status of Vagrant with Vagrantfile
$ vagrant provision	This is used to execute the provisioning commands on a box
$ vagrant destroy	This is used to delete the current instance of the guest; this command will delete the virtual disk and every file along with every setting
$ vagrant box	This is used to handle box commands, such as add, list, remove, and repackage files to delete the current instance of the guest
$ vagrant package	This is used to package the current box environment into a reusable box
$ vagrant ssh	This is used to log in to a running machine using Secure Shell (SSH) with a Vagrant user
$ vagrant plugin	This allows us to manage plugins such as vagrant-omnibus, vagrant-aws, and vagrant-windows that extend Vagrant with more functionalities

Now, in our next step, we will add a box in the Vagrant machine and create a Vagrantfile to get started.

 Vagrant boxes are freely available in a wide variety. We can download a different operating system from https://vagrantcloud.com/.

To add a box, use the following command:

```
vagrant box add hashicorp/precise32
```

You can also uncomment the following line in Vagrantfile:

```
config.vm.box = 'hashicorp/precise32'
```

The preceding command finds the current URL for `precise32` from Hashi Corp (the company behind Vagrant), downloads it, and enables you to receive updates to that box.

The `vagrant box add` command will display the message as shown in the following screenshot:

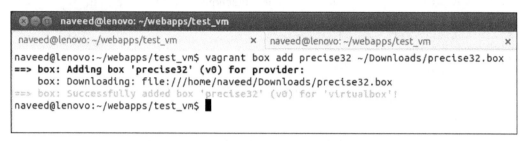

Now, our box has been successfully added. We start this machine and log in via SSH, as shown in the following commands, to make sure that everything is fine:

```
#precise32 is name of box
$ vagrant init precise32
```

This is demonstrated in the following screenshot:

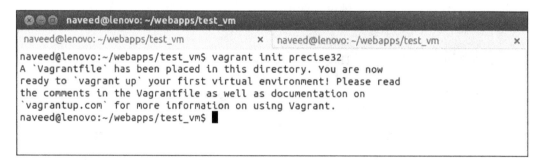

Vagrant created `Vagrantfile` in the same directory. However, before looking into this file, we will start our machine and log in via SSH using the following command:

```
#To start machines
$ vagrant up
```

This is demonstrated in the following screenshot:

```
⊗ ⊜ ⊙    naveed@lenovo: ~/webapps/test_vm

naveed@lenovo: ~/webapps/test_vm              ×    naveed@lenovo: ~/webapps/test_vm              ×
naveed@lenovo:~/webapps/test_vm$ vagrant up
Bringing machine 'default' up with 'virtualbox' provider...
==> default: Importing base box 'precise32'...
==> default: Matching MAC address for NAT networking...
==> default: Setting the name of the VM: test_vm_default_1395495324143_8262
==> default: Clearing any previously set network interfaces...
==> default: Preparing network interfaces based on configuration...
    default: Adapter 1: nat
==> default: Forwarding ports...
    default: 22 => 2222 (adapter 1)
==> default: Booting VM...
==> default: Waiting for machine to boot. This may take a few minutes...
    default: SSH address: 127.0.0.1:2222
    default: SSH username: vagrant
    default: SSH auth method: private key
    default: Error: Connection timeout. Retrying...
    default: Error: Connection timeout. Retrying...
==> default: Machine booted and ready!
==> default: Checking for guest additions in VM...
==> default: Mounting shared folders...
    default: /vagrant => /home/naveed/webapps/test_vm
naveed@lenovo:~/webapps/test_vm$ ▊
```

Now, our test machine is ready. Using SSH, we can log in to a new machine and check whether everything is installed perfectly or not. Now, it behaves like a full-fledged Ubuntu machine. We can use it for several purposes.

```
$ vagrant ssh
```

Using the preceding command, we will log in to a new machine using Secure Shell (SSH) with a Vagrant user.

Under the hood, Vagrant will set up a virtual machine on a local machine. By default, port 2222 of your local machine is used to connect to port 22 of the virtual machine. It generates a private key and keeps it under the `.vagrant` directory. You can add additional settings using the `vagrant ssh.config` command. More detailed information on `ssh.config` can be found at the following link:

```
http://docs.vagrantup.com/v2/vagrantfile/ssh_settings.html
```

Using the `vagrant ssh` command, you will see the following output:

```
vagrant@precise32: ~                         ×   naveed@lenovo: ~/webapps/test_vm            ×
naveed@lenovo:~/webapps/test_vm$ vagrant ssh
Welcome to Ubuntu 12.04 LTS (GNU/Linux 3.2.0-23-generic-pae i686)

 * Documentation:  https://help.ubuntu.com/
Welcome to your Vagrant-built virtual machine.
Last login: Fri Sep 14 06:22:31 2012 from 10.0.2.2
vagrant@precise32:~$ █
```

Once you are logged in to a machine, you can log out using the *Ctrl + D* command.

Executing recipes with Vagrant

Our new machine is ready. Now, we can install Chef-Solo on it, as we discussed in the previous chapter. Even though it is a tedious task, we will cover it smoothly using Vagrant.

Vagrant allows us to automate this process with `Vagrantfile`. We have already created a `Vagrantfile`. Now, let's have a look at the file and execute a recipe with it.

The main object of the `Vagrantfile` is to describe the precise sort of machine needed for a particular task and to explain how to provide configurations and a set of tasks to a new machine. One project contains one `Vagrantfile` that has the footprint of a new machine.

Here, you might be thinking if Vagrant provides us with the basic footprint, why do we need other configuration tools to set up the machine? The main difference is Vagrant can contain only abstract-level tasks, and all activities can be performed in a box, but Chef-Solo has the ability to manage the whole machine. Also, Vagrant is designed to handle virtual machines. The `Vagrantfile` syntax is in Ruby. It's not mandatory to have reasonable knowledge of Ruby. We just need some basic syntax to configure our machine.

As we have already created `Vagrantfile`, if we take a look at the file, it has a lot of commented code inside it. It has a set of instructions that we can configure step by step to customize our machine.

Let's set up some basic configurations and provision our machine.

Provision

Provisioning is a process in Vagrant that allows you to alter configurations, install third-party software, and perform many other tasks with the `vagrant up` command.

We can install software from SSH to any machine, but provisioning allows us to perform the same action in an automated way. For instance, if we want `apt-get update` on every run of the machine, we can easily automate this task using the following code mentioned in `Vagrantfile`:

```
config.vm.provision "shell" do |s|
    s.inline = "apt-get update"
end
```

You can provision Vagrant using the following commands:

- For the first time, `vagrant up` is used. It provisions the new machines; after that, we need to provide the `-provision` flag to provision the machine.

- After modifying `Vagrantfile`, the `vagrant provision` command will serve the purpose.

- The `vagrant reload -provision` command will reboot the machine along with provisions.

Moreover, if you do not want any new provisions on an existing machine, we need to use the `--no-provision` flag.

Let's make some changes in our machine and provision it.

In `Vagrantfile`, uncomment the following line:

```
config.vm.synced_folder "../data", "/data"
```

In the preceding line, the first argument is the actual folder in our operating system, and the second argument is a virtual folder that needs to be created in the virtual machine.

In the previous chapter, we ran the recipe with Chef-Solo. Now, we will run the same recipe with Vagrant box, forward the port 8080 to vagrant 80 ports, and check whether everything works or not.

Move to the `Vagrantfile` Chef-Solo block; it will look like the following code:

```
config.vm.provision "chef_solo" do |chef|
    chef.cookbooks_path = "../data/cookbooks"
    chef.roles_path = "../data/roles"
    chef.data_bags_path = "../data/data_bags"
    chef.add_recipe "mysql"
```

```
        chef.add_role "web"
        # You may also specify custom JSON attributes:
        chef.json = { :mysql_password => "foo" }
    end
```

Now, uncomment the line of `cookbooks_path` and add a recipe line. Once we are done with our Nginx object, we'll look into this.

Create a folder named `cookbooks` one folder up and download the `nginx` recipe from `https://github.com` as shown in the following set of commands:

$ mkdir cookbooks

$ cd cookbooks

$ git clone https://github.com/opscode-cookbooks/nginx

Update the `cookbooks` folder's path in `Vagrantfile`:

```
    chef.cookbooks_path = "../cookbooks"
    # update recipe name in add_recipe
    chef.add_recipe "apt"
    chef.add_recipe "nginx"
```

Please note that Vagrant ships with Chef Version 10, but Chef 10 is already outdated, and all new recipes are compatible with Chef 11.

To install Chef 11, we have two methods. We can either download the box with Chef 11, which is available on the Vagrant box site (`http://www.vagrantbox.es/`) or use the `vagrant-omnibus` plugin to install it.

The omnibus plugin allows us to install any specific version of Chef, or we can write `latest` to download and install the latest version.

For the installation of the `vagrant-omnibus` plugin, run the following command:

$ vagrant plugin install vagrant-omnibus

This is demonstrated in the following screenshot:

```
naveed@lenovo: ~/webapps/test_vm                    x   naveed@lenovo: ~/webapps/test_vm
naveed@lenovo:~/webapps/test_vm$ vagrant plugin install vagrant-omnibus
Installing the 'vagrant-omnibus' plugin. This can take a few minutes...

Installed the plugin 'vagrant-omnibus (1.3.1)'!
naveed@lenovo:~/webapps/test_vm$
```

Now, it's time to open `Vagrantfile` and specify the `omnibus` plugin settings:

```
config.omnibus.chef_version = :latest
```

The preceding line will make sure that the latest version of Chef is installed on our box.

Now, start the machine using the following command:

```
$ vagrant up
```

Before starting the machine, Chef 11 will be installed on our box, and we will see the output with Chef Version 11. However, here, our recipe fails because the dependencies are not being resolved, as shown in the following screenshot:

Let's download all the dependencies and try again.

The dependencies for the nginx recipe are as follows:

- apt
- bluepill
- build-essential
- ohai
- runit
- yum
- yum-epel
- rsyslog

After downloading all the recipes, reload the box again using the following command:

```
$ vagrant provision
```

Provision the box again. The nginx recipe ran successfully. Nginx is ready in the box and is able to receive connections.

SSH to box and check the Nginx service using the following command:

```
$ ps aux | grep nginx
```

You can also check the Nginx service using the following command:

```
$ curl 127.0.0.1
```

It will give out a result, as shown in the following screenshot:

```
vagrant@precise32:~$ ps aux|grep nginx
root      2465  0.0  0.4  10252  1716 ?        Ss   22:38   0:00 nginx: master process /usr/sbin/nginx
www-data  2479  0.0  0.3  10440  1368 ?        S    22:38   0:00 nginx: worker process
vagrant   2745  0.0  0.2   4624   844 pts/0    S+   22:40   0:00 grep --color=auto nginx
vagrant@precise32:~$
```

Nginx installs perfectly. Now, our next task is to forward port 8080 to box 80 connections.

Uncomment the following line mentioned in Vagrantfile, and it will serve the purpose:

```
config.vm.network "forwarded_port", guest: 80, host: 8080
```

Go to `http://127.0.0.1:8080/`, and it should display the Nginx page. Now, we have a complete box ready, with Nginx installed in our operating system.

You can find the complete `Vagrantfile` in the code example.

Creating a Hello World recipe

Now, our next task is to create a simple PHP project, and when we access `http://localhost:8080`, it should display our *Hello World* page.

To do so, we need PHP5 and Apache2.

Now, we can destroy our old box and start a new one with `vagrant up`. Alternatively, we can create a new box with Apache2 and PHP.

Use the same `Vagrantfile` and replace Nginx with Apache2.

Note that Apache2 has the following dependencies. Before we start, we need to clone individual cookbooks into our `cookbooks` folder.

It's a tedious task to clone the repo one by one. In the next chapter, we will use a software tool to resolve the dependencies.

The Apache2 dependencies are as follows:

- `apt`
- `iptables`
- `logrotate`
- `pacman`

Change the Nginx connection to Apache2, remove the old box, and create a new box using the following command:

```
$ vagrant destroy
$ vagrant up
```

The recipes will execute, and we have our new Apache2 box installed. Go to `http://127.0.0.1:8080`, and we will see Apache2's page.

Our next step is to create a PHP project, which can be done as follows:

1. Create a new folder in `cookbooks`:

    ```
    $ mkdir demoapp
    ```

2. The folder structure of the cookbook will look as follows:

    ```
    demoapp
        attributes
                default.rb
        files
                default
                        test.php
        recipes
                default.rb
        metadata.rb
        README.md
    ```

3. Create the folder structure and create files. The important bit of the cookbook is `default.rb`:

    ```
    $ mkdir attributes
    $ mkdir templates
    $ mkdir files
    $ mkdir recipes
    $ touch metadata.rb
    $ touch README.md
    $ touch attributes/default.rb
    $ touch recipes/default.rb
    $ mkdir files/default

    $ touch files/default/test.php
    ```

4. Now, our folder structure is ready. The next step is to create a recipe. First, we will disable the default Apache site. Add the following code block in the `recipes/default.rb` file:

    ```
    apache_site "default" do
      enable true
    end
    ```

In the next step, we will copy the `test.php` file in the `/var/www` directory. The following code block will move the `test.php` file in the `/var/www` directory:

```
cookbook_file "/var/www/test.php" do
  source "test.php"
  owner "root"
  group "root"
end
```

The `cookbook_file` resource will copy the file into the specified location.

After the completion of the recipe, we need to instruct Vagrant to install our `demoapp` cookbook:

```
config.vm.provision "chef_solo" do |chef|
  chef.cookbooks_path = "../cookbooks"
  chef.add_recipe "apt"
  chef.add_recipe "chef-dotdeb"
  chef.add_recipe "apache2"
  chef.add_recipe "apache2::mod_php5"
  chef.add_recipe "demoapp::default"
end
```

Before executing our recipe, we need to set up our environment using `apt`, `dotdeb`, and `apache2` cookbooks. The `mod_php5` recipe is part of the `apache2` cookbook, and it will install every dependency needed for PHP. Then, we can execute our recipe to set up our project in a new virtual machine.

Our first recipe is pretty simple and just responsible for copying one file to a specific location. However, for the complete project, this method is hectic and tedious.

After running the recipe, browse to `127.0.0.1:8080/test.php`, and you should be able to see the PHP file content, as shown in the following screenshot:

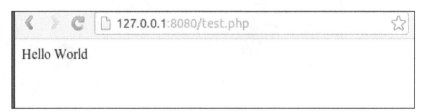

In the next chapter, we will deploy WordPress with PHP and MySQL.

Summary

In this chapter, we discussed virtual machines and different providers. We looked into some different software useful for various operating systems. Then, we installed VirtualBox in our environment.

We installed Vagrant, an automated deployment tool, with VirtualBox, and installed the Chef-Solo plugin to execute our recipes. We created different boxes with different configurations.

We looked at the default Chef version and upgraded our box with the latest Chef version as per the industry standards. Then, we executed some recipes and developed one simple recipe in PHP to get started.

In the next chapter, we will discuss more about cookbooks and the dependency' resolver. Moreover, we will deploy our full-fledged WordPress site using Chef-Solo in the Vagrant box.

4
Developing Cookbooks

We have already discussed the folder structure and some basic content of cookbooks. It's difficult to create folders one by one in a specific manner and create files inside them.

In this chapter, we will discuss cookbooks in detail; we will also discuss how we can avoid errors while developing cookbooks. Chef comes with some handy tools to initialize the folder structures of cookbooks.

In this chapter, we will look at the following topics:

- What is **Knife**?
- The installation of Knife
- **Berkshelf**
- Cookbooks' contents
- Recipes, metadata, attributes, and resources

Exploring Knife

In a Chef infrastructure, Knife runs from the command line and interacts between the Chef server and chef-client. It helps manage cookbooks, nodes, roles, and so on.

As we are working with Chef-Solo, we will use Knife to initialize and download our cookbooks. In an enterprise Chef environment, Knife comes with many handy commands and can be used for managing different nodes and uploading cookbooks, data bags, roles, and much more. A complete list of Knife commands can be found at `http://docs.opscode.com/`.

Also, Chef provides **chef-dk**, which includes all the necessary packages you need to get started with Chef. It includes Berkshelf 3.0 and **Test Kitchen** (an integration testing framework).

There are no extra steps involved in the installation of Knife. Knife is a part of Chef server and gets installed with Chef. As we have already installed Chef on our machine, let's confirm the installation of Knife using the following command:

```
$ knife -v
```

The preceding command will give out an output as shown in the following screenshot:

```
naveed@lenovo:~/webapps$ knife -v
Chef: 11.10.4
naveed@lenovo:~/webapps$ █
```

Developing recipes and cookbooks

Cookbooks are collections of recipes, and contain each step of instructions. As we already have Knife installed on our machine, let's create a basic folder schema for a cookbook. Our goal is to develop a recipe that will install PHP, MySQL, Apache2, and WordPress.

The name of our cookbook is wpblog:

```
$ knife cookbook create wpblog
```

By default, the preceding command will generate the cookbook structure in the /var/chef folder. In case of any other folder path, use the -o flag.

```
$ knife cookbook create wpblog -o <cookbooks_folder_path>
```

The preceding command will yield an output as shown in the following screenshot:

```
naveed@lenovo:~/webapps/cookbooks$ knife cookbook create wpblog -o /home/naveed/webapps/cookbooks/
WARNING: No knife configuration file found
** Creating cookbook wpblog
** Creating README for cookbook: wpblog
** Creating CHANGELOG for cookbook: wpblog
** Creating metadata for cookbook: wpblog
```

Now that we have successfully created a folder structure of a cookbook, let's take a look at it and add some files to get started.

The folder structure of `wpblog` will look like the following screenshot:

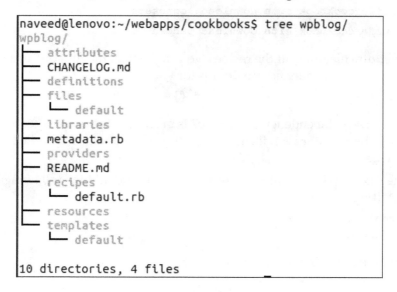

```
naveed@lenovo:~/webapps/cookbooks$ tree wpblog/
wpblog/
├── attributes
├── CHANGELOG.md
├── definitions
├── files
│   └── default
├── libraries
├── metadata.rb
├── providers
├── README.md
├── recipes
│   └── default.rb
├── resources
└── templates
    └── default

10 directories, 4 files
```

As our folder structure is already created, let's create a default recipe using the following steps to execute and create **Vagrant box** to test our recipe:

1. As stated in the previous chapter, create the `vagrant` file and add a new box using the following commands:

    ```
    $ vagrant box add precise32 <box_path>
    $ vagrant init
    ```

2. Edit the `vagrant` file in the same directory and add the box name and cookbook's path:

    ```
    chef.cookbooks_path = "../my-recipes/cookbooks"
    ```

3. Add the recipe name in `chef.add_recipe wpblog` and execute the box.

4. After the execution of these commands, our base box is created with an Ubuntu image. For verification, we can log in to a new box using SSH and check.

5. Now, let's find out some dependencies for our PHP application and download the relevant cookbooks from `http://community.opscode.com`.

    Apache2 dependencies are mentioned in the `apache2/metadata.rb` file:

    ```
    $ knife cookbook site download apache2
    $ knife cookbook site download apt
    $ knife cookbook site download build-essential
    ```

```
$ knife cookbook site download iptables
$ knife cookbook site download logrotates
$ knife cookbook site download pacman
```

6. After downloading all the recipes, you can extract the files one by one, or a simple Linux command can do this for you:

```
$ ls *.tar.gz | xargs -i tar xf {}
```

7. Now, every dependency of Apache2 is present in the `cookbooks` folder. Open the `metadata.rb` file in the `wpblog` recipe and add Apache2 in `depends`.

8. The next step is to create the `default.rb` file and add the following block to install Apache2:

```
#create file cookbooks/wpblog/recipes/default.rb
$ touch default.rb
```

9. Add the following line in `default.rb`:

```
include_recipe "apache2"
```

10. Now, forward the `8081` port to the `80` vagrant and provision the vagrant box using the following commands:

```
# Port forwarding in Vagrantfile
config.vm.network :forwarded_port, guest: 80, host: 8081
# Provisioning the box
$ vagrant provision
```

11. Once the provision is completed, open the browser and type `http://localhost:8081/`, as shown in the following screenshot:

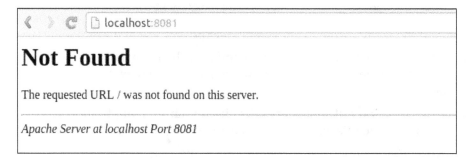

12. Now, Apache2 is installed. The next step is to install some packages in our box and set up Apache with the help of our recipe.

Berkshelf

As we noticed in the previous chapter, it is very difficult to maintain and download the recipes one by one and keep a track of them. Chef comes with the following two plugins that help us overcome this problem:

- Librarian-Chef
- Berkshelf

Both are tools to manage dependent cookbooks.

Librarian-Chef is used to fetch the cookbooks from the central repository and install them using Knife. It's a bundler to resolve every dependency of an application, download, and installation. Also, it has the capability to download public and community cookbooks.

Each cookbook can contain one `Cheffile` and all the necessary information to download the cookbooks.

The following is an example:

```
site "http://community.opscode.com/api/v1"
cookbook "git"
cookbook "timezone", "0.0.1"
cookbook "rvm",
  :git => "https://github.com/fnichol/chef-rvm",
  :ref => "v0.7.1"
cookbook "nginx",
  :path => "/cookbooks/nginx"
```

`Cheffile` is used to download the recipes from Git or any other source. Before the execution of the main recipe, chef-client will download the recipes from sources and install them on a new node.

Berkshelf has almost the same features, but some of them have more advantages than Librarian-Chef. In an abstract level, Librarian-Chef maintains all the cookbooks in a central repository; on the other hand, with Berkshelf, we can easily clone, edit, and upload individual recipes.

The Librarian-Chef command works only in a `cookbooks` folder path (which we specify in `knife.rb`) and looks for the relevant cookbook specified in `Cheffile`; on the other hand, the Berkshelf command works systemwide and can download the relevant recipes.

Working with `Berksfile` is easier than working with `Cheffile`. Each cookbook can contain one `Berksfile`; this means that each cookbook's dependency can be resolved individually. So, we do not need to worry or download the recipes one by one to execute our own recipe.

Before execution of any recipe, Berkshelf will look for every dependency in the `depends.rb` file and download it in the `cookbooks` folder. The folder structure of `cookbooks` will look as follows:

```
wpblog
    cookbooks
        php
        apache2
        mysql
        wpblog
```

After specifying the dependency of `wpblog`, Berkshelf will download each dependency of the individual recipe and execute it on the system. Berkshelf allows us to manage cookbooks as first-class citizens.

Without Berkshelf, the whole procedure of downloading and unpacking cookbooks is difficult and tedious.

The installation of Berkshelf

Before creating `Berksfile` for our recipe, we need to install the Berkshelf plugin for Vagrant. Vagrant has an awesome plugin for `Berksfile`; it works perfectly with Berkshelf.

```
$ vagrant plugin install vagrant-berkshelf
```

The latest version of Vagrant is 1.5.x, and vagrant-berkshelf Version 2.0.0.rc3 is compatible with the latest Vagrant and VirtualBox 4.3. Also, it is dependent on the `geocode` Ruby gem. You can install this Ruby gem using the following command:

```
$ sudo gem install dep-selector-libgecode
```

Please note that if you are using systemwide geocode, Vagrant can cause some problems. It is recommended to use the `geocode` Ruby gem.

The output of a successful installation will look as shown in the following screenshot:

```
naveed@lenovo:~/webapps/test$ vagrant plugin install vagrant-berkshelf --plugin-
version 2.0.0.rc3
Installing the 'vagrant-berkshelf --version '2.0.0.rc3'' plugin. This can take a
 few minutes...
Installed the plugin 'vagrant-berkshelf (2.0.0.rc3)'!
```

The creation of a Berksfile

After the installation of the Berksfile plugin, we will now create Berksfile in our cookbook and list all the dependencies there:

```
# Creation of Berksfile
$ touch Berksfile
```

Once the file is created, paste the following content in Berksfile:

```
source 'https://api.berkshelf.com'
cookbook "apache2", github: "opscode-cookbooks/apache2"
cookbook "wpblog", path: "../wpblog"
```

The syntax is pretty simple; we assigned the source of the Berkshelf API server and set the URL of apache2 from https://github.com/. Similarly, the wpblog path is from the local cookbooks folder.

Now, we can safely delete all the recipes in our cookbooks folder and add the Berksfile path in Vagrantfile. The next step is to mention the Berksfile path in Vagrantfile and remove the cookbooks folder path. As every dependency will be resolved using Berks, we do not need the cookbooks path in Vagrantfile.

Remove the following line from Vagrantfile:

```
chef.cookbooks_path = "../cookbooks"
```

Add the following lines in Vagrantfile:

```
config.berkshelf.enabled = true
config.berkshelf.berksfile_path = "<Berksfile_folder_path>"
```

Now that everything is in place, let's destroy our old box and create a new one with Berkshelf:

```
$ vagrant destroy
$ vagrant up
```

If you notice, during the execution of the recipes, Berkshelf downloaded all the dependencies from Git and placed them in the `cookbooks` folder:

```
naveed@lenovo:~/webapps/test$ vagrant up
Bringing machine 'default' up with 'virtualbox' provider...
==> default: Importing base box 'precise32'...
==> default: Matching MAC address for NAT networking...
==> default: Setting the name of the VM: test_default_1397949514777_14914
Updating Vagrant's berkshelf: '/home/naveed/.berkshelf/default/vagrant/berkshelf-20140420-10108-1qobnuj-default'
Resolving cookbook dependencies...
Fetching 'wpblog' from source at .
Using apache2 (1.10.1) from git://github.com/opscode-cookbooks/apache2.git (at master)
Using build-essential (2.0.0)
Using chef_handler (1.1.6)
Using iis (2.1.0)
Using iptables (0.13.2)
Using logrotate (1.5.0)
Using mysql (5.1.8)
Using pacman (1.1.1)
Using php (1.4.6)
Using windows (1.30.2)
Using wpblog (0.1.0) from source at .
Using xml (1.2.4)
Using yum (3.2.0)
Using yum-epel (0.3.6)
Vendoring apache2 (1.10.1) to /home/naveed/.berkshelf/default/vagrant/berkshelf-20140420-10108-1qobnuj-default/apache2
Vendoring build-essential (2.0.0) to /home/naveed/.berkshelf/default/vagrant/berkshelf-20140420-10108-1qobnuj-default/build-essential
Vendoring chef_handler (1.1.6) to /home/naveed/.berkshelf/default/vagrant/berkshelf-20140420-10108-1qobnuj-default/chef_handler
Vendoring iis (2.1.0) to /home/naveed/.berkshelf/default/vagrant/berkshelf-20140420-10108-1qobnuj-default/iis
Vendoring iptables (0.13.2) to /home/naveed/.berkshelf/default/vagrant/berkshelf-20140420-10108-1qobnuj-default/iptables
Vendoring logrotate (1.5.0) to /home/naveed/.berkshelf/default/vagrant/berkshelf-20140420-10108-1qobnuj-default/logrotate
Vendoring mysql (5.1.8) to /home/naveed/.berkshelf/default/vagrant/berkshelf-20140420-10108-1qobnuj-default/mysql
Vendoring pacman (1.1.1) to /home/naveed/.berkshelf/default/vagrant/berkshelf-20140420-10108-1qobnuj-default/pacman
Vendoring php (1.4.6) to /home/naveed/.berkshelf/default/vagrant/berkshelf-20140420-10108-1qobnuj-default/php
Vendoring windows (1.30.2) to /home/naveed/.berkshelf/default/vagrant/berkshelf-20140420-10108-1qobnuj-default/windows
Vendoring wpblog (0.1.0) to /home/naveed/.berkshelf/default/vagrant/berkshelf-20140420-10108-1qobnuj-default/wpblog
Vendoring xml (1.2.4) to /home/naveed/.berkshelf/default/vagrant/berkshelf-20140420-10108-1qobnuj-default/xml
Vendoring yum (3.2.0) to /home/naveed/.berkshelf/default/vagrant/berkshelf-20140420-10108-1qobnuj-default/yum
Vendoring yum-epel (0.3.6) to /home/naveed/.berkshelf/default/vagrant/berkshelf-20140420-10108-1qobnuj-default/yum-epel
==> default: Clearing any previously set network interfaces...
==> default: Preparing network interfaces based on configuration...
```

After the execution of the recipes, we can see the `Berksfile.lock` file in the same folder as `Berksfile`, and it contains the list of all the cookbooks to be downloaded and installed.

Behind the scenes, Berkshelf downloads the main recipe (in our case, `apache2` is our main recipe) and checks for dependent cookbooks. In our case, as we have seen, Apache2 is dependent on three to four cookbooks. Before the installation of Apache2, Berkshelf will download all the cookbooks and list them in the `Berksfile.lock` file.

The `Berksfile.lock` file will look like the following screenshot after installation:

```
 1  DEPENDENCIES
 2    apache2
 3      git: git://github.com/opscode-cookbooks/apache2.git
 4      revision: 45c0a028c538725b0536160e012c95c35663dcef
 5    wpblog
 6      path: .
 7
 8  GRAPH
 9    apache2 (1.10.1)
10      iptables (>= 0.0.0)
11      logrotate (>= 0.0.0)
12      pacman (>= 0.0.0)
13    build-essential (2.0.0)
14    chef_handler (1.1.6)
15    iis (2.1.0)
16      windows (>= 1.2.6)
17    iptables (0.13.2)
18    logrotate (1.5.0)
19    mysql (5.1.8)
20    pacman (1.1.1)
21    php (1.4.6)
22      build-essential (>= 0.0.0)
23      iis (>= 0.0.0)
24      mysql (>= 0.0.0)
25      windows (>= 0.0.0)
26      xml (>= 0.0.0)
27      yum-epel (>= 0.0.0)
28    windows (1.30.2)
29      chef_handler (>= 0.0.0)
30    wpblog (0.1.0)
31      apache2 (>= 0.0.0)
32      php (>= 0.0.0)
33    xml (1.2.4)
34      build-essential (>= 0.0.0)
35    yum (3.2.0)
36    yum-epel (0.3.6)
37      yum (~> 3.0)
38
```

Now, we do not need to worry about the recipes one by one, and we can easily specify the recipes that we want to install.

Once the installation is finished, open the `http://127.0.0.1:8081/` URL.

The output should look similar to the earlier screenshot. Apache2 is installed perfectly without you having to worry about dependencies.

Understanding recipes

As we have already discussed, recipes are fundamental units of cookbooks and contain step-by-step instructions to configure the machine.

Our goal is to install WordPress, PHP, and Apache2. There are some defined tasks when we install any Linux distribution. The most common task is to update the packages of an operating system. An apt cookbook provides us with the facility to update packages automatically. We will include an apt cookbook to ensure that all the packages are updated.

Open the metadata.rb file in wpblog and add the following dependencies:

```
depends         'rvm'
depends         'apt'
depends         'apache2'
depends         'php'
depends         'mysql'
```

Let's include the php, mysql, and apache2 recipes in our wpblog recipe and provision the machine.

The final code of default.rb will look like the following lines of code:

```
include_recipe "apt"
include_recipe "apache2"
include_recipe "apache2::mod_php5"
include_recipe "mysql::client"
include_recipe "mysql::server"
include_recipe "database::mysql"
include_recipe "php"
```

The apt recipe will ensure that every package on a new machine is updated; the php recipe will install PHP on a new machine, while the mysql::client and mysql::server recipes install the client and server versions sequentially. Similarly, apache2 is responsible for the installation of Apache2. The following command runs any configured provisions against the running Vagrant machine:

```
$ vagrant provision
```

Now that we have our basic toolkit on a new machine, let's first install some packages with the help of resources.

Resources

Resources are a key part of a recipe; they define which action needs to be taken, which files need to be created, and which service needs to be restarted. Resources are responsible for taking any particular action on a node. They are written in a small block of Ruby code that runs sequentially as defined in the recipe. The chef-client looks for a resource, and on successful execution of the resource, it will return the success code to the chef-client. In case of any error, chef-client will terminate the operation and display an error.

As our new machine is ready, let's use some resources and install some basic packages. We will install the `vim` and `screen` packages on our new machine. The `vim` package is used for editing any document, whereas the `screen` package is a multiplexer that allows a user to start multiple tasks inside a single terminal.

Primarily, a resource has four components: type, name, attributes with values, and action. Most of the time, attributes have default values, and they can be used to send notifications to different resources. All the resources share a set of common actions, attributes, conditions, and notifications.

The list of all the predefined resources can be found on the opscode site at the following link:

`http://docs.opscode.com/resource.html`

For installing `vim`, the resource will look like the one shown in the following code:

```
package "vim"
    version "7"
    action :install
end
```

 If you are not sure about the version of `vim`, you can remove the version line and it will install the latest version within the `apt` repository.

As stated earlier, recipes are written in Ruby code. We can loop through a list of packages and install them, or we can mention the resources to install multiple packages one by one. For a cleaner approach, it is recommended that you install various packages in a single resource:

```
%w{
    curl
    screen
    vim

}.each do |pkg|
  package pkg do
    action :install
  end
end
```

The preceding code will install three packages: `curl`, `screen`, and `vim`. Add this resource in `wpblog/default.rb` and provision the box. Once the provision is completed, the mentioned packages will be installed on the new machine and available for use.

As we noticed, the output of `http://127.0.0.1:8081/` is **Not found**. Apache has been successfully installed; now, we need to enable any site in Apache using resource.

Paste the following command in `recipes/default.rb`:

```
apache_site "default" do
  enable true
end
```

The Apache site resource will look for a site in Apache's `sites-available` folder. Once it is found, it will enable the default site. Again, provision the box, and now, you should be able to see the **It Works!** page, as shown in the following screenshot:

Now, we need to create a MySQL database that our application can use. We already included the `mysql` recipe in our `default.rb` file. Let's use the MySQL resource and create a database with a default username and password:

```
mysql_database node['wpblog']['database'] do
  connection(
    :host     => 'localhost',
    :username => 'root',
    :password => node['mysql']['server_root_password']
  )
  action :create
end
```

The preceding code block will create the `wpblog` database with the username as `root` and a root password. We are hardcoding the name of the database in our recipe. It is better if we do not hardcode the database name in the recipe and use it from the `/attributes/default.rb` file. In the next section, we will use a database name and password from the `/attributes/default.rb` file.

Attributes

Attributes are defined in a cookbook and then used to override the default settings on a machine. When chef-client executes, it loads all the recipes and checks for all the attributes in a node. Attributes defined in a cookbook take precedence over the default attributes. The chef-client applies new settings and values accordingly on a new node.

The order of the attributes' precedence is mentioned as follows:

- A `default` attribute declared in cookbook attributes
- A `default` attribute declared in a recipe
- A `default` attribute declared in an environment
- A `default` attribute declared in a role

Now, we will create a database name in our `attributes/default.rb` file and use it in the `mysql_server` resource:

```
# wpblog/recipes/default.rb
Default.wpblog.database = 'wpblog'
# Replace the name of database with attribute, now final resource will
look like this:
   mysql_database node['wpblog']['database'] do
   connection (
:host => 'localhost',
:username => 'root',
:password =>    node['mysql']['server_root_password']
)
action :create
end
```

Provision the box again, and now, MySQL, Apache2, and PHP are ready in our new box. The root user of MySQL is already created with the installation of the database. Now, we will create an application-specific user to perform the `create`, `update`, `delete`, and `select` operations.

Add the following attributes in the `attributes/default.rb` file:

```
default.wpblog.db_username = 'wpblog'
default.wpblog.db_password = 'random_password
```

The following resource will create a MySQL user for the application:

```
mysql_database_user node['wpblog']['db_username'] do
  connection (
    :host => 'localhost',
    :username => 'root',
```

```
    :password => node['mysql']['server_root_password']
  )
  password node['wpblog']['db_password']
  database_name node['wpblog']['database']
  privileges [:select, :update, :insert, :create, :delete]
  action :grant
end
```

The output of the recipe is shown in the following screenshot:

```
Generating chef JSON and uploading...
Running chef-solo...
stdin: is not a tty
[2014-04-20T11:45:18+00:00] INFO: *** Chef 11.4.8 ***
[2014-04-20T11:45:19+00:00] INFO: Setting the run_list to ["recipe[wpblog]"] from JSON
[2014-04-20T11:45:19+00:00] INFO: Run List is [recipe[wpblog]]
[2014-04-20T11:45:19+00:00] INFO: Run List expands to [wpblog]
[2014-04-20T11:45:19+00:00] INFO: Starting Chef Run for precise32
[2014-04-20T11:45:19+00:00] INFO: Running start handlers
[2014-04-20T11:45:19+00:00] INFO: Start handlers complete.
[2014-04-20T11:45:32+00:00] INFO: execute[apt-get-update] ran successfully
[2014-04-20T11:46:34+00:00] INFO: package[ncurses-dev] is a virtual package, actually acting on package[libncurses5-dev]
[2014-04-20T11:46:56+00:00] INFO: execute[a2dissite default] ran successfully
[2014-04-20T11:47:00+00:00] INFO: execute[a2ensite default] ran successfully
[2014-04-20T11:47:00+00:00] INFO: execute[a2ensite default] not queuing delayed action reload on service[apache2] (delayed), as it's already been
queued
[2014-04-20T11:47:01+00:00] INFO: mysql_database_user[wpblog]: granting access with statement [GRANT select, update, insert, create, delete ON `wp
blog`.* TO `wpblog`@`localhost` IDENTIFIED BY [FILTERED]]
[2014-04-20T11:47:01+00:00] INFO: execute[a2dissite default] sending reload action to service[apache2] (delayed)
[2014-04-20T11:47:03+00:00] INFO: service[apache2] reloaded
[2014-04-20T11:47:03+00:00] INFO: Chef Run complete in 103.696743804 seconds
[2014-04-20T11:47:03+00:00] INFO: Running report handlers
[2014-04-20T11:47:03+00:00] INFO: Report handlers complete
```

 If you want to specify any particular listening port on Apache, you can easily do so by defining an attribute in `default.rb`.

An example code for listening port 80 is as follows.

Create the `default.rb` file in `wpblog/attributes/default.rb`:

```
$ touch default.rb
# wpblog/attributes/default.rb
default.apache.listen_ports = [80, 443]
```

Metadata

The metadata of any cookbook is defined in the `metadata.rb` file. It is used to define the basic information of a cookbook, for example, the name of the author, maintainer name, description, version, and most important dependencies. Dependencies are used by Berkshelf to download all the relevant cookbooks from the public or private repository.

Our `metadata.rb` file will look like the following code:

```
name              'wpblog'
maintainer        'YOUR_COMPANY_NAME'
maintainer_email  'YOUR_EMAIL'
license           'All rights reserved'
description       'Installs/Configures wpblog'
long_description  IO.read(File.join(File.dirname(__FILE__), 'README.
md'))
version           '0.1.0'
depends       'apt'
depends       'apache2'
depends       'php'
depends           'database'
```

Summary

In this chapter, we discussed the Knife plugin and how it can be used to create and fetch cookbooks from a site. The creation of files is difficult and tedious. Once we installed Apache2 with recipes, we discussed Librarian-Chef and Berkshelf. We discussed the difference in both tools and started using Berkshelf to resolve dependencies.

The chapter contains the Berkshelf conventions and explains how they can be used with one or many recipes to download dependent cookbooks. We planned to develop the WordPress cookbook with the help of Berkshelf.

After this, the chapter explained the fundamentals of recipes, and with the help of the WordPress cookbook, we discussed each aspect to develop usable recipes.

Moreover, the chapter provides an explanation of attributes, resources, and metadata. We saw the use of resources in many aspects. With the help of MySQL resources, we created the MySQL database and MySQL user which we will use to configure WordPress in the next chapter.

5
More about Cookbooks and Recipes

In the previous chapter, we started developing a WordPress recipe and successfully created a stack with Apache, PHP, and MySQL. We also discussed recipes, attributes, and metadata. In this chapter, we will extend the same recipe and configure WordPress with the help of templates and files. By default, WordPress shows the configuration page to save the settings in the database. With the help of templates, we will create a configuration file with our database settings as defined in the attributes.

In this chapter, we will cover the following topics:

- Files
- Templates
- Roles
- Data bags
- Python/Django cookbook with Nginx and uWSGI
- Restart services with upstream and server handling

Using files

Files are used as a resource to manage files on a new or existing node to create, delete, or update file contents. They contain user and group information along with the permission that needs to be assigned.

The syntax of the files is mentioned in the following code:

```
file "/tmp/testfile" do
  owner "root"  group "root"
  mode "0755"
  action :create
end
```

The preceding code block will be used to create a `testfile` in the `/tmp` folder, by the root user. The `action` attribute specifies the action that needs to be created.

Exploring templates

A template is an **Embedded Ruby (ERB)** file that is used to create configuration files based on variables and logic defined by a cookbook. A template can contain mixed Ruby code or expressions; it provides a great way to manage configuration files on any node.

Templates are used with a template resource, and each resource includes actions, attributes, and file sources. Template resources are very close to file resources; the only difference is that templates are based on Ruby code, and on the other hand, file resources are used to copy files to a particular location.

Templates should have the following two components:

- A template resource, which instructs the chef-client to perform any action
- A template file in the `templates` folder

The folder structure of cookbook templates will look similar to the following:

- `default`
- `ubuntu-12.04`
- `ubuntu-14.04`

If we notice our `cookbooks` directory, we will see that the `templates` folder is already created by Knife. Let's complete our recipe and create a WordPress configuration file with a template.

We will extend our old recipe and add actions to download and configure WordPress. We already created a database and database user in our recipe. Now, the next step is to download WordPress and unzip it.

Here, we will use `remote_file` and the `directory` resource to download the latest WordPress version and copy it to a document root directory of Apache. Let's add the following code block to `wpblog/recipes/default.rb`:

```
wordpress_file = Chef::Config[:file_cache_path] + "/wordpress-latest.
tar.gz"
remote_file wordpress_file do
  source "http://wordpress.org/latest.tar.gz"
  mode "0644"
end
directory node["wpblog"]["path"] do
  owner "root"
  group "root"
  mode "0755"
  action :create
  recursive true
end
```

> The complete documentation of `remote_file` and the `directory` resource is available at the following links:
>
> http://docs.opscode.com/resource_directory.html
>
> http://docs.opscode.com/resource_remote_file.html
>
> Both chef-client and Chef-Solo create a `Chef::Config[:file_cache_path]`, so it is available explicitly. This location is used in several cookbooks, and it is recommended for cached file downloads in recipes because it is a location that is known to Chef.
>
> The `wordpress_file` variable will be used to return the cached path of the WordPress path. The benefit of using `cache_path` is to prevent downloading the same file again and again. WordPress will download Chef and save it to the cache path folder in order to avoid getting it downloaded for every run.

In the previous code, the source is specifying the download path of the WordPress archive, and similarly, `mode` is setting the file permission; the `0644` permission can be used by the owner to read/write a file. The `directory` resource will be used to create a directory in our defined path.

Before proceeding further, we need to define a path in our `wpblog/attributes/default.rb` file:

```
default.wpblog.path = "/var/www/wpblog"
```

Let's unzip the latest WordPress file with the `execute` resource. The `execute` resource is used to execute any Shell script in Chef:

```
execute "expand-Wordpress" do
  cwd node['wpblog']['path']
  command "tar -xzf " + wordpress_file
  creates node['wpblog']['path'] + "/wp-settings.php"
end
```

This is demonstrated in the following screenshot:

```
vagrant@precise32:/var/www/wpblog$ ls
index.php        wp-blog-header.php     wp-includes           wp-settings.php
license.txt      wp-comments-post.php   wp-links-opml.php     wp-signup.php
readme.html      wp-config-sample.php   wp-load.php           wp-trackback.php
wp-activate.php  wp-content             wp-login.php          xmlrpc.php
wp-admin         wp-cron.php            wp-mail.php
vagrant@precise32:/var/www/wpblog$ ▊
```

The `creates` action will ensure that `wp-settings.php` does not execute the same code block again if it already exists in the folder. An alternate `not_if` is also available for the same operation.

Provision the box again, and we can verify our changes using `vagrant ssh` or by typing `http://localhost:8081/wpblog/` in the browser, as shown in the following screenshot:

Now, the next step is to create the `wp-config.php.erb` template and place it in the `wpblog` folder with our database settings. WordPress provides `wp-config-sample.php` by default; we will copy this file to our `templates` folder and add the attributes to replace with actual values.

Also, for the creation of a unique salt (a salt is a secret key that is used to generate hashes to prevent attacks) and generation of a secret key, we will use the WordPress salt generation service (`http://api.wordpress.org/secret-key/1.1/salt/`). If you open the `wp-config-sample.php` file, it is mentioned in comments to generate salt using the WordPress service.

The basic version of the `wp-config.php.erb` file is shown in the following screenshot:

```
3   /** The name of the database for WordPress */
4   define('DB_NAME', '<%= @database %>');
5
6   /** MySQL database username */
7   define('DB_USER', '<%= @db_username %>');
8
9   /** MySQL database password */
10  define('DB_PASSWORD', '<%= @db_password %>');
11
12  /** MySQL hostname */
13  define('DB_HOST', 'localhost');
14
15  /** Database Charset to use in creating database tables. */
16  define('DB_CHARSET', 'utf8');
17
18  /** The Database Collate type. Don't change this if in doubt. */
19  define('DB_COLLATE', '');
20
21  <%= @wp_salt %>
```

Now that our template is ready, let's pass variable values from the recipe, including the WordPress salt and secrets.

Add the following code block to `wpblog/recipes/default.rb`:

```
# Following line will cache the file path of wp-salt.php
wp_salt = Chef::Config[:file_cache_path] + '/wp-salt.php'
if file.exist?(wp_salt)
  salt_file = File.read(wp_salt)
else
  require 'open-uri'
  salt_file = open('https://api.Wordpress.org/secret-key/1.1/salt/').read
  open(wp_salt, 'wb') do |file|
    file << salt_file
  end
end
```

The `file.exist` method will ensure that the code is not executing again; `open-uri` will open the salt service URL, and like the `file` operation, we will read the data and create a new file named `wp-salt.php`:

```
template node['wpblog']['path'] + '/wp-config.php' do
  source 'wp-config.php.erb'
  mode 0755
  owner 'root'
  group 'root'
  variables(
    :database    => node['wpblog']['database'],
    :db_username => node['wpblog']['db_username'],
    :db_password => node['wpblog']['db_password'],
    :wp_salt     => salt_file)
end
```

Now, we will use the `template` resource to read variable names from attributes and send them to the `wp-config.php.erb` file. In `template`, we can pass the variables using the variable in resource, or we can directly print using `node[:wpblog]` `[:database]`.

Save the file and provision the box again. Open `http://localhost:8081/wpblog/`. Now, we can see the WordPress installation page, as shown in the following screenshot:

We have successfully installed WordPress with Chef-Solo; only the configuration of Apache is left. Let's complete the remaining bit with the help of templates and attributes.

Create a new file in `wpblog/templates/default/site.conf.erb` and add the following code, as shown in the following screenshot:

```
 1   <VirtualHost *:80>
 2       ServerName <%= @params[:server_name] %>
 3       DocumentRoot <%= @params[:docroot] %>
 4
 5       <Directory <%= @params[:docroot] %>>
 6           Options FollowSymLinks
 7           AllowOverride FileInfo Options
 8           AllowOverride All
 9           Order allow,deny
10           Allow from all
11       </Directory>
12
13       <Directory />
14           Options FollowSymLinks
15           AllowOverride None
16       </Directory>
17
18   </VirtualHost>
19
```

Now that we have the Apache configuration ready, let's instruct our recipe to use this file and enable our custom site.

The `apache2` cookbook provides the `web_app` resource. With the `web_app` resource, we can enable our custom site in the Apache configuration. A more detailed documentation on the Apache resource is available at the following link:

`https://github.com/onehealth-cookbooks/apache2`

The best practice is to create custom resources and providers inside a cookbook to prevent code duplication.

Add the following code to the `wpblog/recipes/default.rb` file:

```
web_app 'wpblog' do
  template 'site.conf.erb'
  docroot node['wpblog']['path']
  server_name node['wpblog']['server_name']
end
```

As we are assigning `server_name` in the resource, we have to declare it first in the `/attributes/default.rb` file:

```
# wpblog/attributes/default.rb
default.wpblog.server_name = 'wpblog'
```

Also, we need to disable the default site, as we have the `apache_site` resource set to `enable true` in our recipe. Let's change it to `false` to disable the default site, as shown in the following screenshot:

```
28
29   apache_site "default" do
30       enable false
31   end
```

Now that everything is in place, let's provision the box again or destroy the box and create it again to verify everything:

```
$ vagrant destroy
```

```
$ vagrant up
```

Once your recipe is completed, open `http://localhost:8081/`, and the browser output should display the home page of WordPress.

You might be thinking that it's a long installation process to prepare the WordPress node. However, if you have to create the WordPress node on a timely basis, you do not require the same tedious steps every time. Once your recipe is ready, we can execute it, and our new instance is ready to serve the traffic.

Data bags

A data bag is a global variable that is stored in JSON and can be accessed by Chef. It is indexed for searching and loaded by chef-client while executing the recipe.

We can use data bags directly in a JSON file or create them using Knife Solo. First, we will use a simpler approach, that is, updating the password with a JSON file.

Before we proceed further, we will create a JSON file under the same folder of `Vagrantfile` and use this file to run recipes. The benefit of this approach is that Chef-Solo requires a JSON file to execute recipes, and we can test our JSON file with Vagrant. The steps are as follows:

1. Create your file in the same folder where `Vagrantfile` exists:

```
# wpblog.json
{
    "wpblog":{
        "db_password": "dbpass1234"
    },
    "run_list": [
        "recipe[wpblog::default]"
    ]
}
```

2. Comment on the `add_recipe` line in `Vagrantfile` and add the following code block in `Vagrantfile`:

```
chef.json.merge!(JSON.parse(File.read("wpblog.json")))
```

Now, `Vagrantfile` will look like the following screenshot:

```
87      config.vm.provision :chef_solo do |chef|
88    #     chef.cookbooks_path = "../cookbooks"
89    #     chef.roles_path = "../my-recipes/roles"
90    #     chef.data_bags_path = "../cookbooks/wpblog/data_bags"
91    #     chef.add_recipe "php"
92    #     chef.add_recipe "wpblog"
93    #     chef.add_role "web"
94    #
95          chef.json.merge!(JSON.parse(File.read("wpblog.json")))
96    #     # You may also specify custom JSON attributes:
97    #     chef.json = { :mysql_password => "foo" }
98      end
99
```

3. Provision the box again and log in to a new machine using SSH to verify that the new password has been updated:

```
# cat /var/www/wpblog/wp.config | grep WP_PASSWORD
```

The output of the preceding command is shown in the following screenshot:

```
vagrant@precise32:~$ cat /var/www/wpblog/wp-config.php |grep DB_PASSWORD
define('DB_PASSWORD', 'dbpass1234');
vagrant@precise32:~$
```

We can see our new password from the data bag that has been updated. You might be wondering about the use of a data bag in a JSON file as it is saved in the disk space. Imagine that, in a cloud environment, you create a system variable to save the password, but it is not available on the disk space. While executing the recipe, you can retrieve it from a system variable and populate it accordingly in the configuration file.

> An alternate method using Knife is more secure. Knife provides a decent method to create data bags from a command line. Here is an important point to note: if you are using the Chef server, then by default Knife will create the data bags on the Chef server. However, as we are running our recipes with Chef-Solo, we need a few additional plugins to generate data bags and save them locally.

Knife Solo allows you to generate data bags individually without any Chef server integration.

The installation commands for the Knife Solo and Knife-Solo `data_bag` are as follows:

```
$ sudo apt-get install ruby1.9.1-full
$ sudo gem install knife-solo
$ sudo gem install knife-solo_data_bag
```

> As an alternate method, we can use Chef Development Kit (chef-dk). Now, Knife is officially a part of chef-dk.

We will use a data bag for our sensitive information. As per our WordPress recipe, we will use the database password with data bags. Knife Solo supports different encryption methods to encrypt sensitive information.

Data bags can also be created using the following command:

```
$ knife solo data bag create apps wpblog --json '{"id": "wpnlog", "db_password": "newpassword"}'
```

Update the data bags directory path in `Vagrantfile`:

```
chef.data_bags_path = "../cookbooks/wpblog/data_bags"
```

Now, the final version of `Vagrantfile` will look like the following screenshot:

```
87    config.vm.provision :chef_solo do |chef|
88    #   chef.cookbooks_path = "../cookbooks"
89    #   chef.roles_path = "../my-recipes/roles"
90    chef.data_bags_path = "../cookbooks/wpblog/data_bags"
91    # chef.add_recipe "php"
92    # chef.add_recipe "wpblog"|
93    #   chef.add_role "web"
94    #
95        chef.json.merge!(JSON.parse(File.read("wpblog.json")))
96    #   # You may also specify custom JSON attributes:
97    #   chef.json = { :mysql_password => "foo" }
98    end
```

After the creation of data bags and `Vagrantfile`, reload the Vagrant machine, as some of the configuration paths have been changed. It is recommended that you reload the machine once using the following command line:

```
$ vagrant reload
```

Once your machine has been reloaded and provisioned, verify the database password changes using SSH to the virtual machine. Now, the `/var/www/wpblog/wp-config.php` file should have the updated database settings with the new database password.

Moreover, we can use a secret key file to encrypt the data bag information.

An example of an encrypted data bag can be seen in the following command:

```
$ knife solo data bag create apps wpblog -s secret_key
```

An example of an encrypted data bag with the secret key specified in a file can be seen in the following command:

```
$ knife solo data bag create apps wpblog --secret-file 'SECRET_FILE'
```

 Note that the secret file path should be specified in `solo.rb`; otherwise, Chef-Solo will terminate the recipe with an error.

Roles

The term "role" is used to define certain patterns and processes of configuration on a single or several nodes. Imagine that if your application has high traffic and one server is not able to handle all requests, you might need another server to handle requests. You need Apache (or any other web server) across all nodes. In this case, you can create the role name Web Server, and it contains the run list of the Apache server with site configurations. Roles are defined in the same way as the normal recipes with `run_list`. Similarly, we can create a database role to set up a database server.

 Note that the use of roles with the Chef server is controversial. It's fine to use them with Chef-Solo.

Let's have a look at some real-world examples.

Now, we will create a cookbook to set up a Python/Django app with Nginx and uWSGI. We will not explain each bit of code as we did in the previous example, assuming that now we have an understanding of the recipe structure and the important code blocks.

Create a new cookbook named `django_app` and a new Vagrant box to execute the recipe.

Follow the same steps for creating cookbooks and some attributes. Assuming that we have already created the `django_app` cookbook, create a folder named `roles` in the `cookbooks` folder and update the path in the new `Vagrantfile`.

Follow the same instructions to create `Vagrantfile` for a new application and forward port 8082 to the port 80 Vagrant box.

The `Vagrantfile` of the new machine will look like the following screenshot:

```ruby
81    config.berkshelf.enabled = true
82    config.berkshelf.berksfile_path = "/home/naveed/webapps/cookbooks/django_app/Berksfile"
83    # Enable provisioning with chef solo, specifying a cookbooks path, roles
84    # path, and data bags path (all relative to this Vagrantfile), and adding
85    # some recipes and/or roles.
86    #
87    config.vm.provision :chef_solo do |chef|
88    #   chef.cookbooks_path = "../cookbooks"
89        chef.roles_path = "../cookbooks/roles"
90    #   chef.data_bags_path = "../cookbooks/wpblog/data_bags"
91    #   chef.add_recipe "php"
92    #   chef.add_recipe "wpblog"
93    #   chef.add_role "web_server"
94    #
95        chef.json.merge!(JSON.parse(File.read("django_app.json")))
96    #   # You may also specify custom JSON attributes:
97    #   chef.json = { :mysql_password => "foo" }
98    end
```

The contents of the `Vagrantfile` are almost the same; create the JSON file under the same folder and add the following code:

```
{
    "run_list": [
        "role[web_server]"
    ]
}
```

Now, we will create the role of `web_server`.

Under the `roles` directory, create a new file of `web_server.rb` and update the following content:

```
name "web_server"
description "A role to configure nginx web server"
run_list "recipe[apt]", "recipe[nginx]"
```

Now, if you notice that Berkshelf will download the cookbooks before executing the role. Once Berksfile downloads all the recipes, then role will use those downloaded cookbooks. In this case, we need to mention `nginx` in `Berksfile`.

> The dependencies can be declared in the `metadata.rb` file or directly in `Berksfile`. It is recommended that you mention the dependency in the `metadata.rb` file. The `Berksfile` will read the `metadata.rb` file and download the dependencies. Otherwise, we need to mention them explicitly in `Berksfile`.

Now, we add `nginx` in `Berksfile`:

```
source 'https://api.berkshelf.com'
cookbook "apt", github: "opscode-cookbooks/apt"
cookbook "nginx", github: "opscode-cookbooks/nginx"
```

Start the Vagrant box using the following command:

```
$ vagrant up
```

Once it is completed, open `http://localhost:8082/`, and you will see the Nginx page, as shown in the following screenshot:

Additionally, we will use the custom log directory and disable the default site using the same role by performing the following steps:

1. Add the following lines in `roles/web_server.rb`:

```
default_attributes "nginx" => {
    "log_location" => "/var/log/nginx.log",
      "default_site_enabled" => false
}
```

2. Provision the box again, and the default site has now been disabled. Let's start creating our recipe to set up the project. Add the dependencies in `Berksfile`:

```
# Berksfile
source 'https://api.berkshelf.com'
cookbook "apt", github: "opscode-cookbooks/apt"
cookbook "nginx", github: "opscode-cookbooks/nginx"
cookbook "python", github: "opscode-cookbooks/python"
cookbook "user", github: "fnichol/chef-user"
cookbook "django_app", path: "../django_app"
```

3. Add the dependencies list in `metadata.rb`:

```
depends          'python'
depends          'user'
```

Now, our recipe will have the instructions to install a Python virtual environment. Clone the code from `https://github.com` and add the configuration file in the `sites-enabled` folder, as shown in the following screenshot:

```
24  include_recipe "python::pip"
25
26  python_pip "virtualenv" do
27    version "1.10.1"
28    action :install
29  end
30
31  user_account node[:django_app][:user] do
32    ssh_keygen true
33  end
34
35  python_virtualenv node[:django_app][:virtual_env] do
36    owner node[:django_app][:user]
37    group node[:django_app][:group]
38    action :create
39  end
40
41  git node[:django_app][:path] do
42    repository node[:django_app][:repository]
43    reference node[:django_app][:branch]
44    action :sync
45    enable_submodules true
46    user node[:django_app][:user]
47    group node[:django_app][:group]
48  end
49
50  python_pip "uwsgi" do
51    user node[:django_app][:user]
52    group node[:django_app][:group]
53    virtualenv node[:django_app][:virtual_env]
54  end
55
56  python_pip "django" do
57    user node[:django_app][:user]
58    group node[:django_app][:group]
59    virtualenv node[:django_app][:virtual_env]
60  end
```

We have used different resources in the recipe. Initially, we included `python::pip` to install Python packages. Then, we installed the virtual environment Version 10 with the help of the `python_pip` resource. The `user_account` resource belongs to the `user` recipe that we have already defined in Nginx. We are creating one user and a few Python project files under this user. The `git` resource will use to clone the repository from GitHub; the full path of GitHub is defined in the `/attributes/default.rb` file.

We have defined the following attributes in `attributes/default.rb`:

```
default.django_app.app_name = 'django_app'
default.django_app.home_dir = '/home/webuser'
default.django_app.virtual_env = File.join(node.django_app.home_dir,
'django_env')
default.django_app.repository = 'https://github.com/navidurrahman/
django_app'
default.django_app.path = File.join(node.django_app.virtual_env, node.
django_app.app_name)
default.django_app.user = 'webuser'
default.django_app.group = 'webuser'
default.django_app.nginx_conf = 'site.conf'
default.django_app.uwsgi_path = File.join(node.django_app.virtual_env,
node.django_app.app_name, 'uwsgi.ini')
```

Attributes can be defined using two syntaxes. We can either use
`default['django_app']['user']` or `default.django_app.
user`. It's a matter of style which one you want to use.

For detailed information about accessor methods (an accessor method
is used to return the value of a variable), please refer to `http://docs.
opscode.com/essentials_cookbook_attribute_files.
html#accessor-methods`.

While executing the recipe, Nginx will be installed from the `web_server` role.
Now, our `web_server` is completely independent from the `django_app` recipe.
In the next cookbook where we require Nginx to be installed, we can directly use
the `web_server` role to install Nginx.

Similarly, we can separate the database recipe. Roles provide us with a cleaner way
to avoid code repetition.

Execute the recipe using `vagrant up` and browse to `http://localhost:8080`.

You will see the page as shown in the following screenshot:

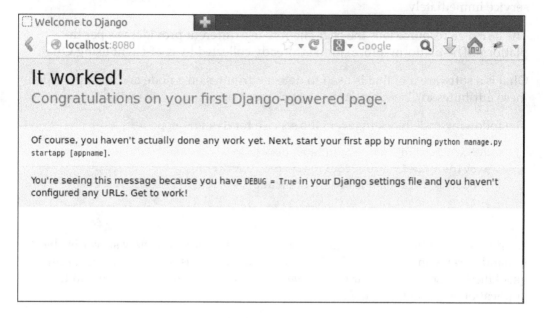

Restarting services and server handling

We have used uWSGI with Nginx to deploy a Django application. A uWSGI project aims at developing a full stack to build hosting services. It has a pluggable architecture to support more platforms, and a common configuration style. To deploy the Django application, we have used the .ini file to save all the configurations of the Python application.

We'll not go into the details of a uWSGI application now. Please refer to the following uWSGI documentation for detailed information:

```
http://uwsgi-docs.readthedocs.org/en/latest/
```

An interesting bit of our recipe is to restart services with an upstream script. A service tells Chef-Solo to use one of the OS-specific providers. First, we create a .conf file in the init folder to handle the service script. Then, the service resource of Chef supports multiple attributes for start, reload, and status commands:

```
template "/etc/init/django_app.conf" do
  source "django_app.conf.erb"
  owner "root"
  group "root"
  mode "0755"
end
```

Once our service gets registered, we will use a `service` resource to start our service immediately.

The `service` resource tells the chef-client to use different providers as per the platform. The platform information is already collected by chef-client using **Ohai**.

Ohai is a software tool that is used to detect attributes on a node and then provide these attributes to Chef-Solo at the start of every run.

The following code block registers the service for `django_app`:

```
service node[:django_app][:app_name] do
  provider Chef::Provider::Service::Upstart
  supports :status => true, :restart => true, :reload => true
  action [:enable, :start]
end
```

At the end, we will start the `django_app` service, and now, our new server is able to handle traffic immediately. The benefit of this service is that if the application gets killed for some reason, it will *respawn* the process again and ensure that the application is up and running.

Now, you have the recipe ready for a Django application. You can create one or more servers within the span of a few minutes.

Summary

In this chapter, we continued with WordPress recipes and looked into the use of files. We also modified the default database settings with templates and set up a new server by providing database information with templates.

We had a detailed discussion on templates, template variables, and also fetched the values from default attributes and data bags. Moreover, we installed tools to work with data bags using Chef-Solo.

After the completion of the WordPress recipe, we started with a Python/Django application recipe and looked at the usage of roles. We then developed the `web_server` role to deploy Nginx and checked out cases that require the deployment of Nginx repeatedly without code repetition.

Finally, we also delved into how our server will be ready and how to restart the service if the application process gets killed for some reason.

6
Chef-Solo and Docker

In the previous chapter, we successfully developed our recipes and tested them with Vagrant. Also, we executed our recipes with Chef-Solo. In this chapter, we will look at another interesting tool for deployment and execute our nginx recipe with Chef-Solo.

We will cover the following topics in this chapter:

- Docker
- Executing recipes with Chef-Solo on a Docker container
- Some recommended practices for using Chef-Solo
- Chef server and Chef infrastructure

Docker

Docker is an open source software used to automate the deployment of any application in a portable and self-sufficient container. It can run virtually anywhere.

Initially, Docker was built on top of **Linux Containers** (**LXC**) and provided a very lightweight container to build and develop applications. In its recent version, Docker has replaced LXC with its own built-in library (`libcontainer`). You can still use Docker with LXC instead of `libcontainer`. It can be tested on a laptop and is scalable on VMs, OpenStack clusters, server instances, or on all of these. The main concept of Docker is to develop it once and run it anywhere. Docker has tooling to make it very easy to distribute and deploy containers. We have had virtualization technology for a long time, but before that, you had to create multiple types of images because every vendor had their own image format, and there weren't tools or central repositories to make it easy to transfer copies of images.

Currently, Docker is in development and very near to production release, but it is worth having a look at Docker. Primarily, Docker is used for the following purposes:

- Automating the packaging and deployment of applications
- Creating lightweight, private **Platform as a Service (PaaS)** environments
- Automated testing and continuous integration/deployment
- Deploying and scaling web applications, databases, and backend services

Before getting started with Chef-Solo and Docker, let's have a brief discussion on how it is different from the traditional virtual box.

As discussed earlier, it is built on a Linux container, which allows Docker to use multiple OS resources, and it has **Advanced Multi-layered unification Filesystem (AuFS)**. The beauty of the AuFS filesystem is that you can have a read-only and write-only part of the filesystem. Also, the containers can share the read-only filesystem with the individual writing part. It means many containers can share the read-only part among each other.

AuFS is a stackable unification filesystem, which unifies several directories and provides a merged single directory. AuFS is the default filesystem of Docker, but other types of storage such as **B-Tree Filesystem (BTRFS)** are also supported by Docker.

Traditional virtual systems did not share their own set of resources and did minimum sharing between each other. The AuFS approach, in this case, makes the LXC very lightweight, and it takes just a few seconds to start a container, and in some cases, less than a second.

If you are looking for a complete virtualization tool, then Docker is not a good choice. We have learned in the previous chapters that we can build new instances with cookbooks and recipes. However, every time the machine boots up, the recipes take some time to boot a new instance, and it needs extra dependencies to configure the system. Comparatively, a Docker image stores itself on the filesystem and does not need any external resources.

Docker provides a decent way to obtain a snapshot of the current operating system. It is an actual implementation of *Write once, run anywhere*. In this chapter, we will create a basic Docker container first, and then, we will extend this container with the help of Chef-Solo.

Installing Docker

Currently, Docker is supported only on 64-bit machines. It requires the 3.8 kernel version to execute properly. If you are using Ubuntu 12.04, upgrade the kernel version first, as precision comes with kernel 3.2 by default.

We can upgrade the kernel version using the following command:

```
$ sudo apt-get install linux-image-generic-lts-raring linux-headers-
generic-lts-raring
```

 You can use the mentioned command on Linux 12.04. Ubuntu 14.04 has the 3.8 kernel Version by default.

The Docker installation can be done using the following commands:

```
$ echo "deb http://get.docker.io/ubuntu docker main" | sudo tee /etc/apt/
sources.list.d/docker.list


# Check that HTTPS transport is available to APT
if [ ! -e /usr/lib/apt/methods/https ]; then
    apt-get update
    apt-get install -y apt-transport-https
fi
# Add the repository to your APT sources
echo deb https://get.docker.io/ubuntu docker main > /etc/apt/sources.
list.d/docker.list
# Then import the repository key
apt-key adv --keyserver hkp://keyserver.ubuntu.com:80 --recv-keys
36A1D7869245C8950F966E92D8576A8BA88D21E9
# Install docker
apt-get update ; apt-get install -y lxc-docker
```

It also provides a Shell script to execute and install. We can use an alternative method to install Docker as follows:

```
$ curl -s https://get.docker.io/ubuntu/ | sudo sh
```

Let's confirm the Docker version using the following command:

```
$ docker -v
```

The output of this command is shown as follows:

```
vagrant@precise64:~$ docker -v
Docker version 0.11.0, build 15209c3
```

Another method to install Docker is to use **boot2docker**, a lightweight distribution based on **Tiny Core Linux** (TCL). It works on any 64-bit system that can run VirtualBox (Linux, OS X, or Windows).

The working of Docker

Docker containers are initially created by a base image. We can pull any image from the Docker main registry (a Docker image server is called a **registry**) and start from that point. Mostly, Linux versions are available on Docker. In short, this repository provides a GitHub-type version control system. We can pull the Docker images, make some changes, and commit these changes to the main repository. Currently, docker.io provides only public repositories, but in future, they are planning for private repositories. You can search for different images at https://index.docker.io/.

There are several articles available online to set up a private repository for Docker. We already installed it on our local machine. Let's pull a basic Ubuntu image and start with a *Hello world* example using the following command:

```
$ sudo docker run ubuntu /bin/echo hello world
```

This is demonstrated in the following screenshot:

```
vagrant@precise64:~$ sudo docker run ubuntu /bin/echo hello world
Unable to find image 'ubuntu' locally
Pulling repository ubuntu
3db9c44f4520: Download complete
316b678ddf48: Download complete
5e019ab7bf6d: Download complete
74fe38d11401: Download complete
a7cf8ae4e998: Download complete
99ec81b80c55: Download complete
511136ea3c5a: Download complete
02dae1c13f51: Download complete
e7206bfc66aa: Download complete
cb12405ee8fa: Download complete
5e66087f3ffe: Download complete
4d26dd3ebc1c: Download complete
d4010efcfd86: Download complete
6cfa4d1f33fb: Download complete
e2aa6665d371: Download complete
f0ee64c4df74: Download complete
2209cbf9dcd3: Download complete
f10ebce2c0e1: Download complete
82cdea7ab5b5: Download complete
5dbd9cb5a02f: Download complete
ef519c9ee91a: Download complete
07302703becc: Download complete
cf8dc907452c: Download complete
hello world
```

The preceding command will look for an Ubuntu image from the local filesystem. If it's not available on the local filesystem, Docker will pull the Ubuntu image from the main repository and run the container.

The /bin/echo path will be used to display the *Hello world* example.

Let's take a look at some basic commands of Docker, which we will use in our examples.

To download a prebuilt image from the main repository, use the following commands:

- $ sudo docker search <Name>: This will ease the pull of Docker images with concise names

- $ sudo docker pull ubuntu: This is used to run the Shell of the image container

- `$ sudo docker run -i -t ubuntu /bin/bash`: This will start the Shell of a Docker container
- `$ sudo docker images`: This is used to list all the docker images

There are several other commands available for Docker. For detailed information about Docker commands, please check the Docker documentation. It contains detailed information about the usage of Docker. Also, an interactive Docker shell will go through the basic commands of Docker available at `http://docs.docker.io/`.

Dockerfiles

As we have seen, we can execute individual commands from the Shell. Docker provides a decent method to invoke several commands and instructs the new container to perform a specific job.

Dockerfiles is a script based on different Docker commands. Each command contains an instruction, and it configures the new machine step by step. It can contain all the information from pulling a repository to starting any server.

They have a clean and simple syntax that makes a file more readable and clear. It is designed to be self-explanatory and allows commenting like other programming languages.

Here is an example of a file syntax:

```
# Comments
command argument argument …
# To echo Hello World
RUN echo "Hello World"
```

Let's create a basic Dockerfile and use the same example of *Hello World* as follows:

1. Add the following content to Dockerfile:
   ```
   # Dockerfile
   FROM ubuntu
   RUN echo "Hello World"
   ```

2. Build the Docker container with the following command:
   ```
   $ sudo docker build -t local/test_docker
   ```

3. Our new container's name is `local/test_docker`, and we will look for Dockerfile in the same folder, as demonstrated in the following screenshot:

```
vagrant@precise64:~/test_docker$ sudo docker build -t test_docker .
Uploading context   2.56 kB
Uploading context
Step 0 : FROM ubuntu
 ---> 99ec81b80c55
Step 1 : RUN echo "Hello World"
 ---> Using cache
 ---> 125df2ed9ce6
Successfully built 125df2ed9ce6
```

4. Now, Docker used the same Ubuntu image in a local repository and created another revision of the image with *Hello World*. Next time, it will start the container within microseconds.

5. Now, we will install Chef-Solo on a Docker image and execute our recipe on it.

Thanks to the open source community, the Docker prebuilt container with Chef-Solo is already available on `Docker.io` at the following link:

`https://index.docker.io/u/linux/chef-solo/`

Alternatively, if you want to build a container from scratch, the following content will serve the purpose. Remove the `Hello world` command and add commands to install Chef-Solo and Berkshelf.

Now, our final Dockerfile will look as follows:

```
Dockerfile

1  FROM ubuntu
2  RUN apt-get -y update
3  RUN apt-get -y install curl build-essential libxml2-dev libxslt-dev git
4  RUN curl -L https://www.opscode.com/chef/install.sh | bash
5  RUN echo "gem: --no-ri --no-rdoc" > ~/.gemrc
6  BEL RUN /opt/chef/embedded/bin/gem install berkshelf
```

Have a look at the following commands:

```
FROM ubuntu
RUN apt-get -y update
RUN apt-get -y install curl build-essential libxml2-dev libxslt-dev git
RUN curl -L https://www.opscode.com/chef/install.sh | bash
RUN echo "gem: --no-ri --no-rdoc" > ~/.gemrc
RUN /opt/chef/embedded/bin/gem install berkshelf
```

This is an alternate method to build an Ubuntu image with Chef-Solo. In our example, we will use the open source image and install Berkshelf to execute recipes.

Let's extend our `Hello world` Dockerfile to install Berkshelf and some additional packages as follows:

```
FROM paulczar/chef-client
MAINTAINER Paul Czarkowski "paul@paulcz.net"
```

As we already know that Chef-Solo requires `solo.rb` and `solo.json` to execute recipes, let's create `solo.rb`, `solo.json`, and `Berksfile` in the same folder, as mentioned in the following commands:

```
# Solo.rb
root = File.absolute_path(File.dirname(__FILE__))
file_cache_path root
cookbook_path root + '/cookbooks'
```

In the following code snippet, we can see that the `solo.rb` file is just setting up the root path of cookbooks:

```
#Berksfile
site :opscode
cookbook 'build-essential'
cookbook 'git'
cookbook 'nginx'
```

Berksfile will resolve the dependency of the nginx cookbook. Also, we require one JSON file to execute recipes, as presented in the following code:

```
#solo.json
{
    "run_list": [
    "recipe[nginx::default]"
    ]
}
```

Keep all the files in the same folder and extend the Dockerfile to execute the recipe as follows:

```
RUN apt-get -y update
RUN apt-get -y install python-software-properties
RUN apt-get -y update

ADD ./Berksfile /Berksfile
ADD ./solo.rb /var/chef/solo.rb
ADD ./solo.json /var/chef/solo.json

RUN cd / && /opt/chef/embedded/bin/berks install --path /var/chef/cookbooks
RUN chef-solo -c /var/chef/solo.rb -j /var/chef/solo.json
RUN echo "daemon off;" >> /etc/nginx/nginx.conf

CMD ["nginx"]
```

Another open source utility, **ezbake**, is extremely useful to pack and run Docker images. However, it requires the installation of a local Berskhelf; it will download the recipes locally and execute a new docker container.

You can find detailed documentation on this at the following link:

`https://github.com/paulczar/ezbake`

Once the Docker container is finished, it will give us an nginx directive so that we can run this process in the foreground.

Run the following command again to build the container:

```
$ sudo docker build -t local/test_docker
```

To run the app, use the following command, where the nginx recipe is running on port 80:

```
$ sudo docker run -d -p 80:80 local/test_docker
```

This is demonstrated in the following screenshot:

 Currently, I have installed Docker in a Vagrant box, and the 8081 port of the system is forwarding to port 80. Once everything is installed, http://localhost:8081/ should display the default nginx page.

Docker is under heavy development, and it's not recommended that you use the in-production version.

You might be thinking: if Docker provides us with a revision control system, then what do we need Chef for?

We need configuration tools to build Docker from the entry point; there are several cases where we need to build the OS image from the start.

Recommended ways to use Chef-Solo

In many cases, we need some default system configuration on many servers. Instead of repeating the same code again and again, it is always better to use **roles**.

As we have an example of web_server in the previous chapter, we can create roles for web servers, databases, and so on, depending on the nature of the infrastructure.

Generally, we come across this scenario when things work perfectly when we are developing applications, but in a live environment, some bugs always show up. Most of the time, these kinds of problems occur because of the inconsistent behavior of the production and staging environments. It is true that we cannot overcome all the issues with Chef, but we can avoid the problems by checking for issues at every step.

The following two methods are usually implemented to develop cookbooks and recipes:

- **To finish the application and start writing the recipe**: The problem with this approach is that during the development of an application, you install various packages on your staging machine. You either add in some documentation to track changes or memorize the step. If your application is dependent on many OS packages, it means that you have spent a good amount of time finalizing the recipe.

- **To develop the recipes step by step**: The ideal approach to overcome the problem is to develop your recipe as your application evolves. For instance, we have already decided that our application needs at least nginx with the MySQL database.

Here, we will discuss another tool, Test Kitchen. It has a simple workflow that stresses on speed but optimizes for the freshness of your code that executes on the remote systems between tests. It has a static, declarative configuration in a `kitchen.yml` file at the root of your project.

Detailed information of Test Kitchen can be found at `http://kitchen.ci/`.

Here is another blog post that shows us how to use Test Kitchen with Docker:

```
http://www.timusg.com/blog/2013/10/15/testing-cookbook-with-docker-
and-test-kitchen/
```

We can start developing our applications in a folder. Create a new box with a Vagrant folder and sync the project code folder to a Vagrant box.

Install the nginx recipe on a Vagrant box and forward the port to a new box. On each commit, our code automatically moves to a new box and Nginx displays a new box. To install any new package, extend the recipe and provision the box again. While using this approach, we can develop our recipe with no extra time, and once our application is ready, we can immediately test it on our virtual box.

Do not repeat it. If any recipe can be used further, it is always recommended that you create a new recipe and include it.

The benefit of this approach is to keep the recipes isolated, and it can also be used in future.

Chef server

Chef server facilitates with a quicker way to deploy a complete environment instead of any single machine. We have already discussed that with Chef-Solo, we can configure any single machine. As our infrastructure grows, it becomes difficult to handle operations. Configuration management tools are designed to manage a large infrastructure with several machines.

Chef server is a hub of configurations, cookbooks, node information, and policies. Metadata describes each registered node that is managed by chef-client. Nodes ask chef-client for configuration details from the Chef server. Recipes, templates, and file distributions are saved on the central Chef server. Moreover, Chef server provides an API to send and receive configuration details on the fly.

There are mainly four components of Chef server shown in the following diagram:

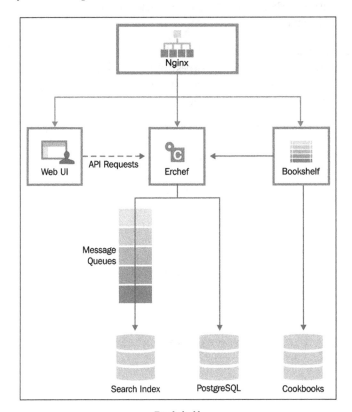

Bookshelf

Bookshelf is used to store cookbooks and resolve the cookbook's dependencies. If any cookbook or a file is declared twice, Bookshelf keeps track of the file and saves the item only once. All cookbooks are stored in flat files, and it is completely isolated from Chef server and search index repositories.

All items are stored in a centralized repository.

Web UI

Web UI is built in Ruby on Rails 3.0, and it has the web interface for Chef server. It contains a list of all the clients, workstations, and so on. We can create clients from Web UI using different settings.

Erchef

Erchef is another name of the Chef server API of Version 11. As Chef 11 is rewritten in Erlang, the purpose of Erchef is to make it more fast and scalable. The API is compatible with Ruby, and all the previous cookbooks written for lesser versions of Chef 11 will continue to work.

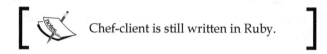 Chef-client is still written in Ruby.

Message queues

RabbitMQ (https://www.rabbitmq.com/) is used as a message queue system for Chef server. To update any item on the main cookbooks, Chef is added into the queue first before the search repository. A message queue is used for asynchronous tasks; it has a publisher-subscriber method to handle tasks.

Chef-expander is used to pull the messages from Rabbit-MQ; these messages are processed and then posted to Apache **Solr**.

Apache Solr is used to index and expose the REST API for Chef server.

Nginx is used as an HTTP server and frontend load balancer.

PostgreSQL is used as a data storage for the Chef repository.

In our examples, we have used **knife** to create cookbooks. In Chef Infrastructure, knife offers a lot more than basic cookbook creation. We can create servers and delete and send custom commands to individual nodes.

While using Chef-Solo, we need some cronjobs (scheduled tasks) to update the server, or we can use some other tool such as Fabric for orchestration.

Another major benefit of using Chef server is the ability to search nodes in the whole infrastructure. For example, the load balancer can update the new servers automatically by searching for servers in the infrastructure. Chef-Solo is meant to manage one machine at a time, but with Chef server, we can send queries such as *all nodes with less than 8 GB RAM*.

If you want to try Chef server without installing it, you can sign up for a free account on Chef Inc. The first five nodes are free to use.

A detailed documentation of Chef server can be found at `http://docs.opscode.com/`.

Summary

In this chapter, we looked at a modern operating system imaging tool, Docker. We also discussed some of the use cases of Docker and how it can help us manage different versions.

After this, we built Docker with the help of Dockerfile. Once we achieved this, we used an Nginx recipe to build the Docker container and bind the port `80` of the main machine to a Docker image.

We also glanced at some recommendations of using Chef-Solo; these recommendations explain certain advantages and disadvantages of using Chef-Solo in different methods.

Then, we discussed Chef server by looking at its basic components and benefits.

There is still much more to learn about Chef server, and you can continue on the topic with any Chef server reading material.

Index

benefit 96
components 94
documentation 96
Erchef 95
Message Queues 95
Web UI 95
Chef-Solo
about 7
comparing, with chef-client 7, 8
configuring 29
prerequisite 22, 23
recipes, executing 30, 31
using, ways 92, 93
cloud node 9
cookbooks
about 10, 23, 50
attributes 24
folder structure 24
metadata 63
used, for additional configuration setup 10

D

data bag 15, 72-75
DEB file
download, URL 36
Debian package management (dpkg) 22
Docker
about 83, 84
installing 85
installing, boot2docker used 86
using 84
working 86, 87
Dockerfiles
about 88-92
creating 88, 89

E

Embedded Ruby (ERB) 66
Erchef 95
ezbake 91

F

files
using 65, 66

files folder 25
folder structure, cookbooks
about 24
attributes 24
files 25
recipes 25, 26
templates 27, 28

H

Hello World recipe
creating 45, 47
Hosted Chef version, Chef 6

I

installation
Librarian-Chef 53, 54

K

Knife 7, 49, 50, 74, 95

L

Librarian-Chef
about 53
installation 55
Linux Containers (LXC) 83

M

metadata 63

N

network node 9
nginx recipe
dependencies 44
Node data storage 7
nodes
cloud node 9
network node 9
physical node 9
virtual node 9

O

Ohai 82
Omnibus installer
  about 22
  advantages 22
  disadvantages 22
Open source Chef version, Chef 7
Opscode 21

P

Parallels
  about 35
  URL 35
Persistent attributes 8
PHP WordPress
  setting up, prerequisite 15
physical node 9
Platform as a Service (PaaS) 84
Private Chef version, Chef 6
process virtual machine 34
provisioning process, in Vagrant
  about 41-44
  commands, using 41
Python/Django application
  with MySQL 16

Q

QEMU-KVM 35

R

RabbitMQ
  URL 95
recipes
  about 11, 58
  developing 50-52
  downloading 29
  executing, Vagrant used 40
  writing, rules 11
Recipes folder 25
registry 86
resource
  about 12, 13, 59-61
  coding convention 13

directory resource 13
Git resource example 12
types 13
roles
  about 13, 76, 92
  declaring 13
  description attribute 13
  name attribute 13
  real-world examples 76-79
  run_list attribute 13
Red Hat Package Manager (RPM) 19
Ruby gem
  Chef, installing as 20
  installing, command 54
Ruby Version Manager (RVM) 20

S

Search indexes 7, 8
server
  handling 82
service
  restarting 81, 82
solo.rb file 29
system virtual machines
  about 34
  Parallels 35
  QEMU-KVM 35
  VirtualBox 34
  VMware 35
  Windows Virtual PC 35

T

templates
  components 14, 27, 66
  exploring 66-72
  folder structure 66
  using 66
terminologies, Chef
  attributes 14
  cookbooks 10
  data bags 15
  node 9
  recipes 11
  resources 12, 13
  roles 13

Thank you for buying
Configuration Management with Chef-Solo

About Packt Publishing

Packt, pronounced 'packed', published its first book "*Mastering phpMyAdmin for Effective MySQL Management*" in April 2004 and subsequently continued to specialize in publishing highly focused books on specific technologies and solutions.

Our books and publications share the experiences of your fellow IT professionals in adapting and customizing today's systems, applications, and frameworks. Our solution based books give you the knowledge and power to customize the software and technologies you're using to get the job done. Packt books are more specific and less general than the IT books you have seen in the past. Our unique business model allows us to bring you more focused information, giving you more of what you need to know, and less of what you don't.

Packt is a modern, yet unique publishing company, which focuses on producing quality, cutting-edge books for communities of developers, administrators, and newbies alike. For more information, please visit our website: www.packtpub.com.

About Packt Open Source

In 2010, Packt launched two new brands, Packt Open Source and Packt Enterprise, in order to continue its focus on specialization. This book is part of the Packt Open Source brand, home to books published on software built around Open Source licenses, and offering information to anybody from advanced developers to budding web designers. The Open Source brand also runs Packt's Open Source Royalty Scheme, by which Packt gives a royalty to each Open Source project about whose software a book is sold.

Writing for Packt

We welcome all inquiries from people who are interested in authoring. Book proposals should be sent to author@packtpub.com. If your book idea is still at an early stage and you would like to discuss it first before writing a formal book proposal, contact us; one of our commissioning editors will get in touch with you.

We're not just looking for published authors; if you have strong technical skills but no writing experience, our experienced editors can help you develop a writing career, or simply get some additional reward for your expertise.

Creating Development Environments with Vagrant

ISBN: 978-1-84951-918-2   Paperback: 118 pages

Create and manage virtual development environments with Puppet, Chef, and VirtualBox using Vagrant

1. Provision virtual machines using Puppet and Chef.

2. Replicate multiserver environments locally.

3. Set up a virtual LAMP development server.

Fast Data Processing with Spark

ISBN: 978-1-78216-706-8   Paperback: 120 pages

High-speed distributed computing made easy with Spark

1. Implement Spark's interactive shell to prototype distributed applications.

2. Deploy Spark jobs to various clusters such as Mesos, EC2, Chef, YARN, EMR, and so on.

3. Use Shark's SQL query-like syntax with Spark.

Please check **www.PacktPub.com** for information on our titles

www.ingramcontent.com/pod-product-compliance
Lightning Source LLC
Chambersburg PA
CBHW060157060326
40690CB00018B/4149